This Time

Leslie Thomas was born in Sou... parents died he and his younge... orphanage. Aged sixteen, he bec... paper in Essex and then did his l... the Communist bandits war. *The Virgin Soldiers* tells of these days, it was an immediate bestseller and has been made into a film with Lynn Redgrave and Hywel Bennett.

Returning to civilian life, Leslie Thomas joined the staff of the *Evening News*, becoming a top feature writer and travelling a great deal. His second novel, *Orange Wednesday*, was published in 1967. For nine months during 1967 he travelled around ten islands off the coast of Britain, the result of which was a lyrical travelogue, *Some Lovely Islands*, from which the BBC did a television series. He has continued to travel a great deal and has also written several television plays. He is a director of a London publishing house. Among his hobbies are golf, antiques and Queen's Park Rangers Football Club. His other books include *Come to the War*, *His Lordship*, *Onward Virgin Soldiers*, *Arthur McCann and All His Women*, *The Man with the Power*, *Tropic of Ruislip*, *Stand Up Virgin Soldiers*, *Dangerous Davies*, *Bare Nell* and *Ormerod's Landing* all of which are published in Pan.

Leslie Thomas
This time next week

With Illustrations by Graham Byfield

Pan Books London, Sydney and Auckland

First published 1984 by Constable and Co Ltd
This edition published 1971 by Pan Books Ltd,
Cavaye Place, London SW10 9PG
19 18 17 16 15 14 13 12 11
© Leslie Thomas, 1964
ISBN 0 330 10700 3
Printed and bound in Great Britain by
Richard Clay Ltd, Bungay, Suffolk

DEDICATED

to my mother and father
wherever they may be
in the hope that, by this time,
they have made it up

1

ONE THING ABOUT living on a hill, there was always lots of sky to see and when you weren't busy you could study it. Sometimes the clouds would race along like lean, white lions; like heraldic lions on the shields of knights I used to think.

Sometimes they were grey and fat and slow. Old elephants pushing each other.

I used to watch that sky a lot when I was a kid. Watch it from under the knobbly tree at the top of the mud-patch. Or, in winter midnights, through the long pane of glass behind my bed, the only bit of glass in the whole of the window.

Boz, in the next bed, had cardboard and squares of black curtain stuck over his window because it had never been put in after the bombing. Some nights he used to creak over in bed and whisper: 'What the 'ell are you looking up out there for? You're always doin' it.'

I never had an answer. It was no good me saying about the lions, or the elephants, or the chases under the moon, or the reassuring stars. Even if I had known how to put words the way I put my thoughts, which I didn't, Boz would have thought I had gone mad.

Boz was the first boy I knew in Dickies. Sometimes he was called Cherry or Shinybright because he had a red nose. He was an enterprising character, a great pincher of bread, a raider of orchards in season. He had once run away from the Home and had been at large for sixteen days, which was a record.

When I think about it all now, it is often Sunday that is the focal point of my remembering. On Sundays the Gaffer would wear his green, hairy suit, perching like a patriarch on his chair at the top of the dining hall, while we slurped our mud cocoa and the cracking of Sunday eggs was as sharp as shooting.

Some things you could be completely certain about on Sundays. There would be a hundred and fifty eggs boiled in a

7

pillow case and you each got one at breakfast; you also got an individual egg boiled for you on your birthday, unless the cook forgot, in which case you had to wait until the next year.

Another Sunday thing was butter beans and pale cold meat for lunch, and potatoes steamed in their froggy skins. In the afternoon Matron would waddle into the chapel and talk about Jesus and thieving, and keeping clean in mind and body, and how her old boys used to write and say how much they had enjoyed it at Dickies. With normal luck that was the last we saw of Matron until the following Sunday.

The Gaffer was different. He was always there. His Sunday speciality used to be to warn us of swift and terrible vengeance if anyone was caught reading the *News of the World*. This retribution was presumably to come from him, although he intimated that it might easily arrive from God. Anyone found smoking would be struck by lightning.

After Matron's sermon on Sunday afternoon, the Gaffer would pick us out two or three at a time to be allowed out for walks. Those who sat up straightest on their benches were the first to go. If he had it in for you then you probably did not get out at all.

We nearly always went to Richmond Park. There were fine full trees there, and bracken and small hills and a pond, and American soldiers and their girls. We used to run there, buy the *News of the World* and share it out amongst us.

Each Sunday evening the vicar would wheel in on his bike. We would pick out our favourite choruses and nearly always end up with 'Jesus wants me for a sunbeam,' or 'He has blotted them out.' Once a German flying bomb scraped the roof and exploded when we were right at the crescendo of the chorus. He nearly had a hundred and fifty sunbeams just then. That was the night I first noticed how very old the Gaffer was.

He was not a man you could love, the Gaffer. But, after these years, I think of him with a deal of affection and some reverence because he was a good man in his narrow way. He was growling and grey, thin and with a slight stoop as the years went on, although he would never surrender to them, pushing his shoulders back and tautening his backbone whenever he discovered they had crept up on him.

8

If the stoop was slight, his cynicism was large. He was entitled to it. Forty of his sixty-odd years he had occupied with boys. Thieves and angels; dopy, dull, brilliant, trustworthy, skulkers and workers, happy and sad and sneering, helpless and horribly capable. But all boys. The Gaffer had, by the time I became one of them, an all-embracing distrust of anything in short trousers.

I remember the first day I saw the Gaffer and Dickies. It was in March and I had been thirteen a few days before. It was a day that held on to the tail of winter. An empty day with rain on the pavements and in the trees and in the sky. A small, pointed wind blew the rain into my face as I shuffled along from the station beside the man who had brought me.

The man did not talk. I kept up with him. I was carrying a blue sack, like a pillowcase, over my shoulder and it contained very nearly all I had in the world. The big houses in Gloucester Road stood vaguely behind their misty trees.

Towards the end of the road there shot up a sudden high wooden fence and I knew we had almost arrived. A few more shuffles and there was the gate. The man turned in and I followed.

Then I stopped. It may have only been for seconds, because the man was walking on. But I know I stopped and looked up at it. A quick loneliness came over me like a pain. No boy has ever felt so much by himself as I did in that moment.

I am not going to pretend that the years that followed were hard, or cruel, or even unhappy. This was not so. This could never be an Oliver Twist story or it would not be true.

But standing at the gate, in the drizzle, and the man walking ahead up the path unconscious that I had even stopped, left me afraid and wondering what was going to happen to me from then on.

The place filled the horizon. Yellow bricks and blank windows; a tower at the centre capped with a pointed roof, a horror built, it seemed, from some architect's nightmare. Across the front of the building were the words 'The Dalziel of Wooler Memorial Home' blazoned in golden letters, of all things, like an advertisement. In the middle of the tower, in more modest gold, was 'Dr Barnardo's Homes'.

I jerked myself to some sort of movement and followed the man who had brought me. He went up some stairs in the foot of the tower and I went in through the door after him.

We were in an entrance hall reeking of floor polish. There was a boy standing there picking his nose. The man told him to go and fetch Mr Gardner, the superintendent, and he went.

The man stood a couple of yards away looking around him. Drippings from our coats made liquid explosions on the red floor and settled like small rubies at our feet. The man still did not look at me, or speak. I might have been by myself.

Down the corridor echoed the Gaffer. He turned the corner of the hall into our view and approached with military stride and granite expression. He shook hands with my escort, a brisk once-up-and-down, and then led him into the office.

I remained there, still damp with rain and unhappiness, resting my blue bundle on the floor, and crooking a parcel of books in my other arm. With two fingers of this hand I hooked on to a small package holding a tin half-full of toffees. The full tin had been sent to me by an elder brother, just after my mother died, with instructions that half of the sweets were for me and the other half for my younger brother. I never heard any more from the elder brother, and I did not see the younger brother for another year and a half. Despite wretched and returning temptations I never ate the sweets. I kept them for him.

Standing in the hall was a little like being at the entrance to a temple, but with your nostrils full of floor polish instead of incense. Bootfalls and distorted calls sounded from the landing up inside the tower.

A few yards from where I stood there was a pedestal topped by a marble bust wearing a layer of dust and a slightly annoyed expression. There was quite a lot of dust clogging the inside of the eyes and I attempted to cheer my miserable self by trying to imagine what would happen if the head came to life and found all that muck in its eyes. I don't know who the head was – or if I did, I have forgotten – but the gentleman in the picture on the wall, the one with the watch-chain and the lion-tamer moustache, was Dr Barnado, the Father of Nobody's Children.

It was odd really, I suppose, that I should be standing there. It seemed only a few dark nights before that my mother had read to us (not for the first time) the jerking melodrama of a London orphan called Wops the Waif. A chapter or two of this was sufficient to ensure that both my brother and I went to bed booing copious tears, and praising Providence that we were so much more fortunate.

We had gentle beds, and cornflakes in the morning, and friends, and a roof. And there was poor old Wops, all holes and icy toes, fighting life and death from a gutter.

Wops was the prototype of the scrags that Barnardo pulled into the rough warmth of his charity. And here was I, on this March day, one of Wops' successors.

There was another photograph on the wall, perched just above the latitude where the grim green paint finished and the grim cream paint began. This picture, like the Barnardo one, had taken on a tone of autumnal brown. It was of a mild-looking lady whose giant hat seemed to be forcing her head down into the drowning depths of a huge fur. I don't know who she was either.

Under the picture now stood the boy who had been sent to fetch the superintendent. His mission accomplished, he had returned to busily exploring his nose. I did not know it then, but he was Boz.

''Ow old are you then?' he inquired solicitously.

'Thirteen – last week,' I said. 'Wednesday.'

He appeared to make some mental calculation. 'You'll be gettin' fourpence, then,' he said eventually.

'Fourpence? When?'

'Saturdays. That's if 'e don't stop it,' he replied, nodding towards the Gaffer's office door. 'Saturdays we get the dush.'

'What's dush,' I asked stupidly.

'Wot I've just said,' he repeated patiently. 'Dush is money. Pocket money, see? You'll get fourpence. Some kids here get a tanner. And them that's in the band get more than that.'

'There's a band?' I said, brightening.

'Yeah,' he grinned. 'But you can't get in it till you're fourteen and you've got to learn the bagpipes or the bells. But they get more dush.'

Then I put the big question. 'What's it like?' I asked.

He knew I meant the place. 'Dickies?' he said. ''Orrible. Bloody 'orrible. Worse 'ome I've ever bin in.'

Having given this assurance, Boz then welcomed the tortoise arrival of another boy. A boy wearing a foully greased blue jersey; a boy with three teeth missing, all in the front; a boy with hair thickly plastered down with a substance I later learned was stolen lard. The boy's name was Breadcrumb George.

He had gained this unusual appellation through his habit of gathering all the breadcrumbs from the table, piling them up and sweeping this harvest into his mouth with a deft movement. He for ever claimed that he didn't know he was doing it.

Breadcrumb George was carrying a large tin with floor polish mixed in it like strawberry ice cream. The mixing had been done with a stick which was now projecting from the middle of the red mess.

'Got the splosh,' said Breadcrumb George briefly, without looking at me, and dragged on down the corridor. Boz, who had apparently been awaiting his arrival, turned with him, saying to me: 'We're on chapel.'

Off they went, presently followed by a smaller, mild-looking lad, wearing steel-rimmed glasses, and bearing two large pieces of folded blanket. This boy was called Bosky because he was cross-eyed.

They went into a big room at the end of the corridor. At the far end I could see a wooden cross standing out against a bright blue cloth draped across the wall. Whatever the sanctity of the place (I discovered later that this was reserved for Sundays) it had no apparent restraint as far as Boz and his workmates were concerned. Boz took the stick, dipped it deep into the polish, and, moving backwards along a broad strip of brown lino, banged dollops of red at frequent intervals.

When he had accomplished this he stood at the far end of the lino strip, under the cross, and Breadcrumb George shuffled to the end nearest me. The pieces of blanket which Bosky had borne were folded and Bosky himself sat solemnly cross-legged on them.

Breadcrumb gave him a push and he slid on his blanket-sledge along the lino, spreading out the polish with his journey.

At the other end Boz swung him expertly around, and then propelled him back. Back he went, and back again. As they went thus lightly about their task, so the trio sang. I have never forgotten that song. It was simple, but sad in a way, although

13

they would never have thought it so. Nevertheless it was a song of hope and of remembering.

Their song went:

> '*This time next week,*
> *Where shall I be?*
> *Sitting by the fireside*
> *Scoffing my tea.*
> *Plenty of comics,*
> *Lots of books,*
> *No more matron's dirty looks . . .*'

It was a lusty thing, and a song of hope, unconscious perhaps, or nearly so, because each of us grew with a small and usually diminishing dream that one day we would find our own home again and be restored to it. And it was a song of remembering for those of us who had known such a home – once anyway.

There was an accepted tradition that, at least once during your term at Dickies, you should try and reach that former home. It was a sort of journey to Mecca, a compulsive demand that had to be met, a tradition glorified by a thousand unlikely stories and adventures.

The more resourceful were at large for many days. One journeyed on the buffers of a goods train, it was rumoured, to Yorkshire.

Running away was called 'doing a bunk,' and when your energy and ideas were exhausted it was a calculated policy to surrender to the police at about midnight. In this way you ensured a sympathetic supper before going to sleep in the police station, and a beneficial breakfast the next morning before being returned to retribution. Some boys were veteran bunkers, working around the police stations like travellers on a circuit, and receiving thus a variety of suppers and breakfasts, without raising the suspicions of the coppers.

The sad fact about the genuine runaways, the first-timers, not the boys who made a career of it, was that, often after a journey of some difficulty, they eventually reached what they remembered as their home, only to find that it was no longer theirs.

They may have recalled the place only mistily, from a distant time, remembering perhaps only the town and district, and having had to feel their way from there to the street and eventually the house. And when they got there they were strangers and nobody knew them. The mother who had given them up may have gone away a long time before. In the street the people had changed. There was no one to take them in. After all the journey they were alone again.

Adventure was always bubbling at Dickies. If you were not plotting an escape there were other things.

A stroller in Gloucester Road, one red twilight in summer, was shaken by the alarming sight of a boy in pyjamas climbing steadily across the top of the high golden letters across the jaundiced front of the home. He tore in to report what he had seen. The Gaffer took the news with reasonable calmness because nothing ever surprised him now.

He politely thanked the informant and strode quickly and efficiently up the stone stairs for three floors. His timing was magnificent. He reached the top dormitory window just as the boy was going past outside. Without fuss the Gaffer grabbed him and pulled him in. The boy forcefully denied he was trying to die, and added that he was just on the point of winning a tanner bet.

Boys there were in infinite variety. We had Spanish kids, black-eyed left-overs from the civil war; darkies (one with ginger hair) from Accra and Cardiff. We had some boys who were a bit simple and some with the flashing spark of genius.

There were kids who wouldn't wash; kids who were capable of lifting anything from anybody anywhere; kids who could sit at the piano and play Chopin. Some used to swear and some pray with rivalling fervour; some were crazy about railway engines, and some had an advanced preoccupation with women.

We had one boy who used to sit like a monk, unspeaking and unspoken to, reading, reading, reading. We had another who had all the makings of a master crook, but who lay in the dark dormitory at night and spun a web of breathless adventure as lyrical and as versed as a young Stevenson.

2

EVERY NOW AND then my father would blow home from sea and break a few windows. He used to smash the windows, generally at the front of the house, because my mother wouldn't let him in. She said they were legally separated and nothing was going to change it.

One day the mistress of the cub pack to which I belonged came past on her bike. At the next cub meeting she asked me how the windows came to be broken.

'It was a bomb, miss,' I said desperately. 'A small German bomb. Right in the garden.'

There had been a smattering of air raids that week, so I thought this was plausible. Baden-Powell and his cubs' promises about truthfulness were, for me, temporarily suspended as an emergency measure. The cub mistress, an earnest, glassy young woman with the strange name of Miss Rabbitt, goggled behind her lenses.

'Oh dear,' she said. 'Your poor mother! We must all go around and see if we can help her.'

'No,' I cried. 'Mum's in hospital. The bomb blew her arms off.'

My old man was stoking boilers in ships' stomachs for most of his life, journeying the world, again and again, searching for whatever sailors search for. He had a funny, agile face with a habit of looking around corners with his mouth and his eyes. His sins were whist drives and whisky.

We hardly ever saw him, but what time he was at home my mother decided was too much. He had a weakness for getting drunk and giving his money away. Sometimes, for variety, he would take up a lost cause in a dockside pub and challenge someone twice his size to a fight. He frequently arrived home plastered (in both senses) and bandaged from his waist to his spreading ears.

On the other hand, I think he loved us dearly in his way. When he sauntered home from his far wanderings he would bring strange toys for us, Roy and myself, and gentle, fragile

china, as light as paper, for my mother. This was before their legal separation. My mother would accept with reserved gratefulness the Japanese coffee set, or the tea set from Macao, wash it tenderly and set it proudly with her collection on the Welsh dresser.

Then three nights later the old man would spoil himself, come home raving from the Dock Hotel, and be turfed out once more. When a bomb demolished the Dock Hotel he took us all down to see the ruins. There we were, mother impatient to get home and probably feeling that Hitler had at last achieved something good; Roy and I, in our raincoats, wondering that so many bricks could have gone to make one building; and dad, his eyes groping over the debris in eloquent sorrow. Other men were standing along the pavement in the same stunned, homeless way.

The old man had been a sailor almost from the time he left school, with a break during the first war when he was a soldier. His two elder sons had gone to sea in their teens and had risen, by study and endeavour, to the bridge, while dad doggedly shovelled on in the boiler room. He spent half his life in that steaming hell and I have heard it said that nothing was too heavy nor too hot for him. My only prayer for him has been that he was not down there when the torpedo hit his ship.

In his young days he brought despair to his father, a moustached Welsh Baptist and a Liberal too, and to his gentle mother, by disappearing for months or even years. Then one deep night they would answer the door and he would be there arrayed in a gaucho's outfit he had won in a poker game in South America.

Once he jumped a ship in Australia and adventured for the goldfields to strike his fortune. Six months later he was in a seaman's hostel in Sydney, broke as a beggar, and a sea captain said he wanted a sailor for a voyage back to England. Jim Thomas willingly put his name on the line and the next morning found the ship.

'Jesu,' he used to say when he was telling the story, 'there she lay and I couldn't believe what I saw. There's me been a stoker ever since I could lift a shovel of coal and this thing was all masts and rigging like a spider's web.'

The schooner took six months of horror and hurricane to get home. My old man, hanging tightly somewhere high in the rigging, reckoned he wept most of the way.

Looking back over the valley of these years it is a strange realisation to me that I seem to know so much more about my father than my mother. Yet it was she who was with us all the time.

She was a small woman, pretty even in her late forties. She was fond of quoting, sentimentally, miracles like the Angels of Mons, or how the singing of 'Eternal Father' brought succour to the crying crew of a wrecked steamer off the Glamorgan rocks, as proof that there was a God. But in my memory I can never recall her entering a church.

Her unreliable husband, and the fact that her two eldest sons frequently vanished to distant seas for years and never bothered to write or send money, had led her to expect nothing from them.

This was all she normally received. Her life was a tired serial of house-cleaning jobs, with a spell as a school cleaner and another as a factory sweeper thrown in for variety. One thing was constant; there was never any money to spare.

The first and last time I can remember my parents embracing was in 1938. The year I recall exactly not because the fact that they kissed was such a significant event, unusual though it was, but because of the reason for the kiss.

In Spain the civil war was rolling. My father and my elder brother were involved (on opposite sides, I believe) but strictly in the cause of cash. They were on gun-running ships. The old man's vessel was in Barcelona harbour when an adventurous dive bomber appeared over the housetops and dropped a high explosive bomb right down the funnel.

Coldly the announcer on the BBC news said that all the crew were dead. It was a Newport ship and the curtains were drawn in many streets. My mother did not cry but she hardly said anything all the day. Then from the remote BBC came further news. Some of the men had been picked up. The announcer read the names and my father's was the last one on the list.

He came home, all bandaged up as usual but at least

honourably this time. My mother and he crushed together and he let out a yell because she pressed on one of his fractured ribs.

About this time he travelled to Barry to his father's funeral and came back maudlin drunk. He was arrested as he left the train at Newport station (on the opposite side to the platform) and, not having any money, was kept in custody overnight. A policeman came to tell us what had happened and all the boys in the street wanted to know why he had gone to our door. I told them my old man had committed a murder and was being hanged next morning in Cardiff prison.

My mother had grumbled all the way to pay the fine on that occasion, and I think it was from then on that their relationship began to wither drastically. In the early days of the war when he came home from sea he was sullen and angry and she spiteful and unforgiving. There were the window-smashing episodes and bitter, black rows, while we children cried and tried to pull them apart.

During their stormings they often wished each other dead, each asserting, in premature triumph, that the other would go first. As it was their deaths were quite abrupt and in their proximity almost poetic.

From the spring of 1939 to the late summer of 1943 we lived in a district of Newport called Maesglas, which in Welsh means Green Fields. All reasons for the name had diminished to a joke as the docks spread on the black coast, and as the railways and the mean houses followed them.

All the houses were in unremitting terraces, blindly facing each other across the street, frequently smoke-capped by the emissions of the neighbouring engine sheds.

It was a district of trudging husbands, black from their work, of fat and skinny women and tribes of children; of summer pavements clouded with dust and lamp-post games on gritty winter nights. There was a working men's institute, a church made of corrugated iron, and an aromatic fish and chip shop that was an agony of fighting kids every night from Monday to Saturday.

There *were* green fields, but in the distance, lying on their sides up a minor ridge of hills. My mother used to do housework at a house on top of the ridge. Sometimes she wore a red coat and when I came home from school I used to stand on the air-raid shelter and pick her out, bright as a ladybird, coming down over the fields, and I would put the kettle on.

She used to make us happy, as far as she could. Every summer we used to get new plimsolls – dappers we called them – go pounding down the pavements like young horses with white hooves. Every winter there were new Wellington boots and plenty of rain to go with them. In the sharp of December and January we went to school warmly wrapped in woollen bala-clavas, scarves and mittens, knitted by earnest ladies every-where for our brave merchant seamen. My father would bring them home, and my mother accept them on the basis that they were gifts for the children and not her.

Quite apart from these strictly utility things he was always generous with his coming-home presents. Secretly Roy and I used to hope that there would be a period of mild skirmishes between dad and mum, before the actual fighting, so that he would have time to distribute the gifts.

Once, before they were separated, he came home empty-handed. His presents had been filched, but he took us into the town the next day and said that Roy and I could choose what we liked. We elected to have a dozen day-old chicks and nothing would nudge us from the choice.

Mother called the old man all sorts of silly fools when we got home. She pointed out the fairly obvious fact that we had no hens and therefore no means or hope of rearing the yellow chicks. But, to her credit, she tried. They were put in a box in front of the fire and then in the bath smothered in a jungle of straw. The last two died while mum cuddled them to her be-neath the blankets of her own bed.

In the dark kernel of another night, again before the separa-tion, the old man sailed in from a voyage with a hard slab of frozen kippers. He was a bit drunk and he arrived at our back door with this small ice floe and announced: 'When Jim Thomas eats – everybody eats!'

These were scraping times and all the neighbours were glad to share the kippers with us. The whole district hung with the sweetness of their frying that day. My father, who claimed they had been given to him, took on a look of wrinkled worry and wondered if the police would investigate the cause of the sudden sea-harvest.

In the autumn of 1942 my mother became ill and one evening she was taken into hospital. I remember it like a sequence in one of those shadow theatres, where the shapes flicker all around the sides of a drum.

All sorts of people came around. Mum was upstairs and she sent down a message about where Roy and I could find our clean pyjamas, because we were going to the hospital with her.

All the people sat like conspirators against the walls downstairs, and although we must have had the light on, I can only think of them as shapes and shadows. They crouched and gossiped, as people do, of other occasions when people had been taken ill and how so-and-so had gone to bed on a Christmas afternoon and just died. Death and hospitals and operations, and the possibilities of ghosts and the Hereafter, enthralled them until the ambulance came. But for some reason not one of those shadows ever offered to take myself and my brother in.

I do not blame them, for they must have had worries and families of their own, even though they could afford to spend an entire evening in macabre reminiscence. Later, nearly a year later, when the time came for Roy and I to go away for ever, they were still of the same sympathy and the same reluctance.

The first time, Roy and I were allowed to stay in the children's ward at the hospital for a few days. Then we had to gather our things, journey down to the women's ward to see woolly-coated mum, before being taken to our first experience of a home.

A strange word. Home. Say it one way – just 'home' – and it is the warmest syllable in the language; deep as a hearthrug, satisfying as dinner, assured as love.

But add one letter, call it 'a home' and, in imagination, immediately, all the deepness and warmth are gone, as though a big door had been opened and a wind had howled in.

It was to a home we went that autumn day. We were there

only three weeks and I recall little of it. The pictures that do come back are of a great, chunked table, scrubbed white as whalebone, standing on the flagged floor of the kitchen; there was a black, open range, and a girl with a leg-iron who jolted around and shouted and laughed a lot.

Two women were in charge of the place, one the daughter of the other. The daughter had a baby which she used to feed at her big breast and she seemed to consider it a good thing that we should see her doing it.

The home was on the forehead of Stow Hill which takes the road from Newport up towards the valleys. On the sharp mornings we used to get up at seven and I used to stand by the window, as though on a cliff-top looking down on the spire of the town hall and the streets all flooded with mist.

The town-hall clock would boom up to me like a lonely bell-buoy rolling in some early estuary. Outside the window the trees in the garden dripped quietly and I shivered as I dressed.

One good thing about this place was that I was able to attend my usual school. Having passed an exam I had moved from the school at Maesglas to one in the centre of town which was four times as old and twice as crowded.

But here they taught you French, which was a considerable academic achievement from the status point of view, and must have been worth hearing considering it was mimed in the accents of pure Welsh dockside.

The lady who taught French was short and rounded, with a beautiful face and a bust like a perfumed pillow. It used to undulate grippingly as she demonstrated the aspirates. I was madly in love with her. One day she set us an exercise to complete and then sat down at her desk and sobbed quietly throughout the lesson. I trembled with hot thoughts of what I would do to the man (which I concluded was the trouble) if I ever caught him.

Unfortunately my devotion missed her completely. In fact her physical softness was a contrast to her brisk manner and occasional turns of thorough nastiness. One day she told us to shut our eyes and recite a verb from memory. So lost was I in the contemplation of my adored that I missed the instruction.

23

While the remainder of the class plunged themselves into darkness and incantation, I sat goggling stupidly at her lovely face.

For the first time she looked directly at me. She left her desk and came to me up the aisle. My breath seemed to fill my whole body. She was next to me now: that perfume vibrated. I looked up at her. She brought back her arm and gave me a wham on the side of the head that knocked me down between the desk and the floor.

Our mother was out of hospital and home again after about three weeks. We went home. For a few weeks, or perhaps it was months, she was well again, and we began making plans for the holiday we were going to have in the country the next summer.

In February my father turned up. There was a hopeful sort of half-reconciliation between them. It was a streaming day, gutters gushing, and I came home from school through the rain and found him sitting by the fire with a cup of tea.

I heard them talking about the war. He had seen men die in the acid sea, a rope's length away. He had seen ships suddenly blossom red and orange in the awful darkness and then watched the flower of flame sucked into the water. Men, he had seen, covered in oil and burning.

He leaned towards my mother, gave her his cup and, I remember this so well, he said: 'Dolly, let me come back. I've got to have somewhere to go when I come home.'

She did not answer right away. She took the cups into the kitchen, washed them and let their one chance of a last brief happiness slide down the drain with the water. 'Let me think it over,' she said when she came back. 'Wait till you come home next time.'

He went back to his lodgings. Then, the day before he sailed again, he came to the house. He did not stay long. But those few minutes are still bold and black and white in my mind. So clear are they that I might have known that this was to be the last time.

Just before he went, Roy was sitting one side of the small bay window and I was the other. Mum was on the couch.

Dad kissed Roy and then he came across to me and did the same. He had a hard, bristly chin and mouth, and he was clumsy when it came to affectionate gestures. Then he went over to mother and gave her a jerky kiss and a pat on the cheek and said something like: 'Next time, then.'

Then he did one of his round-the-corner grins or grimaces, I don't know what they were, and walked out into the street. A month or so later we had a rare letter from him, posted in Freetown, Sierra Leone. I don't remember what it said; to my shame I was more interested in getting the stamps before my brother did.

A week on, and a rosy busybody who used to come and read my mother's fortune in the tea-leaves and in the cards arrived, and I heard my mother whisper something to her. I heard the woman say: 'The cards foretold it, Dolly, didn't they?'

That night, when we were in bed, mum told us that the old man was drowned.

His ship, the SS *Empire Whale*, split by a torpedo, went down in the South Atlantic. I believe that all the men went too.

A few years ago they put his name on the Merchant Navy Memorial on Tower Hill. I went up there to look at it. It is near the bottom of a column catalogue of fifty who drowned with that ship. It just says 'D. J. Thomas.'

The sea-birds sit on the stone like guardians; the ships sigh in the Pool of London; and the clerks and young girls from the City offices sit in summer on the grass across the way. And he lies, dead, but peaceful anyway, in the ocean.

I once asked someone in a Whitehall office if they could give me the details of the sinking of the *Empire Whale*. They came back with the bald date and the latitude and longitude, and that was all they knew about Jim Thomas and the end of his life. I don't suppose you could expect them to know much else.

Five months after he had gone, my mother was deeply ill. Early in September I woke up one morning to hear her crying. I went into her and she said that Roy and I would be going away that day – so that she could go into hospital.

'It's a school,' she said. 'Down in Devon. The masters play soldiers in the woods and the fields with the boys. I've

25

heard they have a very good time. But you will write, won't you?'

Just like that. One minute – or one hour anyway – we were ordinary kids at home – and then we were packed and leaving, having kissed and wept with her by her bed.

And that was the last we ever saw of her.

3

A DEEP-THROATED creek comes in from the sea at Hope Cove, turns through the red and green fields of the South Hams, and finally collides, head-on, with a stone wall at Kingsbridge.

Now, the place is a pretentious little holiday goldmine, all boats and bed and breakfasts. The same petrol light lies across the water like a cloak at seven on an autumn evening, but now there is always a gaze of visitors to tell each other how lovely it is.

Then it all had a wartime quiet about it. The backwater was quite derelict and unused. Along the banks of the creek the air in the dusk used to have an acrid taste and there were fireflies, not ice-cream wrappers, on the water.

A mountainous high street, called Fore Street in the West Country manner, has its base at the stone wall which stops the creek. It climbs between the shops that used to provide the needs of a small market town, but are now loaded with Devon jugs and Cornish pixies and other journeying junk, past the church with the funny epitaph at its door, and eventually to the crown where there is the police station and a house that was once painted white and green.

It has a garden wall with trees frothing over the lip, a cobbled courtyard and stables. It has three lawns, falling away gracefully, in steps or stages, and all around the lawns, like spectators, stand shrubs and bushes and lean trees.

In the strange way that things like gardens, or houses, or sometimes people, have of shrinking between the time when you saw then as a child and when you see them again as an adult, the house and the garden seemed to have diminished when I went back a year or so ago.

It was to this house that I and my brother went the day after we left our mother. We had spent the first night in Cardiff, taken there by a woman from some welfare office. We had to meet a man on the station.

A train journey to us was sufficient to lift us from the misery of leaving home. Cardiff was only twelve miles but we had never been there. The train retraced the journey we had taken from home to the station that morning, crossing the bridge over the River Ebbw from where we could pick out the roof of our house. The river, like black treacle, wound through its coal-dust banks and we could see the places where we had many times gone down to dig out buckets of Ebbw coal. A bucketfull of coaldust from the river, dried out in the back garden, always saved us having to buy the stuff.

South of there the marshes spread, green and calm, and the ships in the docks on the horizon seem to be sailing on a sea of grass.

'How will we know the man we have to meet at Cardiff station?' I asked, looking at the ships on their meadow ocean.

'Oh,' said the lady, whoever she was. 'We'll know him because he will have a blue Dr Barnardo's Homes badge in his lapel.'

This was the first moment that we knew where we were bound.

Our mother had told us the encouraging lie of the 'school' and no mention of Barnardo's had been made until then.

Now it came like a cold hand on the neck, the realisation that we were destined for *a* home, another one, and this time a distant place and with the prospect of a much longer stay. How long, we did not realise then.

It is easy enough to blame a woman for sending her children away in this manner. But she knew, if everyone else thoughtfully denied it, that she had cancer and was surely dying. There was virtually no one to whom she could look for help. In the years before the war she had alienated herself, after a long series of quarrels, from both her own and her husband's families. She distrusted a good many other people, and did not want to 'put upon' others. Neighbours had plenty of children of their own, and she knew that caring for us was no longer the matter of a temporary assignment.

Who knows how many hollow nights she lay in pain and worry, wondering what she could do with us? In the end she took the brave step of sending us to an institution. It was brave, for it must have broken her heart after the long struggle she had fought. Who can blame her? Not I.

The man who met us was wearing the blue badge. He took us to the home in Cardiff and we spent the night there. My brother cried and I stood in the small garden and looked through some little trees at the traffic moving towards Newport on the road outside. It was a low wall and I wondered whether I ought to get Roy and make a run for it now while we were still comparatively near home.

At that time I had an odd idea that somehow my mother had been tricked into sending us to the home; that she had really *thought* we were going to a boys' school where they played soldiers in the woods and fields. It seemed that the right thing to do would be to run back and tell her what they had done to deceive her. But then I remembered her morning tears that day and realised that she had not been tricked into anything. It was us. It had to be like that.

The lorries slid by behind the outspread fingers of the trees heading towards our home. The Cardiff Road went by the bottom of our street. In half an hour they would be near. I wondered how she was, how sick she was. Then I turned away and went back into the home. She knew all right.

On the following day, as though fate were trying to torment us, we saw our house again. Taking us to Cardiff was merely some organisational device and we left there by train, through Newport, to Bristol and down to the West Country. We stood at the window as we went over the iron bridge across the Ebbw again and picked out the roof of our house behind the engine sheds. It was a chilly day. All the chimneys in the street were smoking except ours.

But we were only boys and once the train had burrowed under the Severn, and we began to reach new and unknown places, our sadness was pushed away by the eagerness of exploration. The eternal tightness of money in our family had meant that we had never travelled far. These dipping fields, these amiable towns, these rivers and copper trees were all part of a strange new country.

At Newton Abbot – the peculiar foreign names! – we changed and a homely push-and-pull engine took us down a gentle canyon to Kingsbridge in the South Hams district. Someone – a young woman I think – had escorted us on the journey and with her we walked from the station up the steep of Fore Street.

There were clouds resting on the hill, their bellies swollen with rain. It began to splatter just as we reached the front door and rang the bell.

So this was the first real stop. The first resting place on a nomadic wandering that we both experienced until we were grown enough to decide for ourselves where we would live. It was a solid, country house, the sort that sits contentedly by the side of many a road throughout England. It had a softly carpeted hall and a splendid curving staircase, but we only used the hall for hymns and prayers in the evening, and the staircase, never. We went up the back way.

This was a reception home and it only had twenty or so children. Somewhere I have a photograph snipped from a pink magazine which shows us all standing, one behind the other, rising like steps. There were boys and girls; I am the third from the tallest, Roy is somewhere in the middle and in the front is a weeping and pathetic two-year-old, topically called Winston.

On the first day they did not send us to the school. Instead we were told we could go for a walk. So we bought some apples and then went down to the head of the creek and made boats out of wood we found in the shallows and the mud. It was very quiet down there; a man came up on the deep water in a thin boat and there were some swans and ducks on the far side pushing each other under the old wall.

When I thought it was time to go Roy was in the water up to his knees. He turned and waded out. He dried his legs on my handkerchief. Then he said: 'We ought to be able to get 'ome for Christmas, din' we?'

29

'Yes,' I said. 'I 'spect so.'

There was more sun left in that summer. It browned the harvest, and baked the ground, and made dogs pant up the hill. After we had been at Kingsbridge two weeks we had another three weeks off from school, the usual thing in Devon for many of the children came from farms and were required to help with the crops.

We wandered the fields, watching the men at the threshing, getting in the way, trying to help, hypnotised at the death-chase of dog and rabbit in the gold. The pale boys from the overcast streets ran in the stubble and drank rough-edged cider from the mugs of the labourers. Breathless, every day, we went back to the house and had tea in the big flag-stoned room with the solid table that was like the one in the first home. After prayers we used to write every night and tell our mother what we were doing. And the letters were piling up on the doormat of our empty house many miles away.

There was a wide paddock at the bottom of the garden and beyond that a plank bridge over a leaf-clogged stream, a barren orchard and three pig-sties. They had not been used for a long time, and they were fresh and the sun made the bricks and stones and the old straw smell dry. We went down there one Saturday, several of us, made bows and arrows from the trees, and built a small fire to fry the sour, dried apples. All day the orchard was Sherwood Forest and we the snug outlaws in our settlement.

We went back to tea and it was peanut butter. I remember I had just started when the door from the garden opened and the superintendent stood framed there, beckoning to me. He was a big man, rather handsome, with greying hair. I got up and went across the floor. At first I thought he was going to tell me off about playing in the pig-sties. But he smiled as I reached the door and asked me to go out into the garden. Then I knew what it was about.

We walked towards a place where a lot of autumn flowers were out. There was a stone, round like a loaf of bread. He stopped and put his foot on it. So far we had walked just a few paces and he had not said anything. But I knew what he was going to say because I had dreamed about her in the night and she had been dead in my dream.

'Your mother,' he started. 'She was very ill and in a lot of pain. But she's out of the pain now. She's dead.'

The crimson and yellow flowers fused for a moment in my tears. I can never see a flower lying in the shallows of a stream or blossoms behind a wet window pane without remembering it.

'I dreamt she was,' I said. 'Last night.'

I don't think he knew how to go on from there. He was very good. 'I think I will leave you here,' he said. 'Go in for your tea when you feel like it.'

I walked down the garden, across the thick brown tufts of the paddock, and into the barren orchard. There were the pig-sties where we had been so happy that day. I stirred the place where we had lit the fire to see if it was still alight. It wasn't. In all I think I only cried for about five minutes.

They had a pony called Pomerse and three dogs, Patch, Brutus and Judy, at this house. Pomerse belonged to the superintendent's son but I used to pretend he was mine.

Every evening I cleared out his soggy stable, and then sat in the lamplight working saddle-soap into the sweet leather of the harness and saddle, and shining the brasses.

The pony was black, only half broken-in, as flighty and irascible as a spoilt child. But I learned to ride him, with and without a saddle. Every afternoon, late, after school, I used to take him to the paddock and get on his back. When it was bare-back I would hold his ears firmly in my hands and lie across his pounding neck as we raced over the dying grass. Never had I known that you could fly like this. When he went we never touched the ground and we flung aside the wind in our race.

The superintendent's son was not all that keen on the pony, even though it was his. Many times it was left to me to exercise him. Sometimes we went out of the paddock, clipping up the darkening lanes, and then out into the free country, riding wild in the short evening. He was a fine, fighting pony. Many times he threw me headlong and once, having flung me down breathless on the grass, he deliberately stepped forward and cracked my ankle bone with his hoof.

The three dogs were a comedy team. Patch was a yapping terrier, small and short on temper and wind; Brutus was medium and brown and guileless; Judy a Great Dane, a huge, arched bitch, with slobbering chops but a gentle nature. Taking all three for a walk at the same time was attempting the impossible. Judy would leap ahead with poetic strides that carried her clear and clean from the ground, Brutus would be somewhere about your feet, doing his honest best to keep up. Patch would be half strangled by his collar as you pulled him along behind, yelping and snarling at Judy to cut the pace.

One night towards the close of the year I took the dogs out in the moonlight with John, who was the oldest boy in the home. My brother had gone into hospital with appendicitis the day after I had been told of my mother's death. While he was in hospital he got diphtheria and then something else, so he was there for months, and all the time he thought that his mother still lived.

John and I had become good friends, and on this night we took the dogs up the climbing fields towards the night and its rising moon, I had the two smaller dogs and John was being towed along by Judy. They all ran hard in the cold air and we enjoyed it with them, feeling our boots crunching through the ploughed land, throwing up the earth, and then thudding softly through the soaking grass.

We went howling over a gate, and then through the thin legs of a copse, and eventually to the crest of the fields where we stood with the panting animals looking out over the pale earth.

Then the dogs began to cry and pull. I looked around and standing full under the moon was a giant of a horse, a white stallion, snorting the air. We ran, the dogs ran, more frightened than us I think, and after us came the thundering stallion. That was a bad couple of minutes. I stumbled in the grass and then John tripped and wobbled.

'Let the dogs go!' I hollered as we plunged in panic.

'And run!' he called back, going like mad himself. 'Run or the big sod will 'ave us.'

The dogs flew off over the field, faster than any hunt pack on the most enfiring scent; Judy going like a super-greyhound and the others tearing faster than they had ever gone before. We reached the gate not that long·after the dogs and five seconds in front of the stallion. The sky and its stars raced beneath us as we flung ourselves head first over the bars.

Behind us the drumming had reached a crescendo and then rolled to a stop as he reached the gate. He stood there, his white nostrils up, snorting and steaming. We kept running, because you couldn't be really sure, and the dogs had disappeared through the hedge into the farther field.

They were waiting for us at the next gate, wagging their tails and looking a bit embarrassed at their fright, and probably ours too. We caught up the trailing leads and laughed all the way home along the silver road.

There are not many moments you can choose from your life when you have known utter happiness. But that was one.

Half-way down Fore Street there was a pack of old shops, huddling under a wooden canopy like elderly men beneath an umbrella. One of the shops was the boot repairer's and another was that of Mr. Palk, a pink barber, obese, beaming, and booming, who sang and recited and chatted while he indiscriminately chopped lumps off your hair.

At the side of the shops a pile of steps went up to the church, and at the churchyard door was buried a man who I would like to have met. This could not have been arranged because he had been under there for a couple of centuries, but his epitaph was splendid logic.

One of the status symbols of his day, it seems, was to be buried inside the church. You paid to lie in the porch, or the aisle, or, if you could afford it, in the chancel. Only the peasants ended up under the churchyard grass. But this man had been buried at the door and his engraved message relating this piece of chilly snobbery included the words:

> *'Here lie I by the churchyard door,*
> *Here lie I because I'm poor,*
> *The further in, the more you pay,*
> *But here lie I as warm as they.'*

33

As I knelt in the impossible pew on Sundays, I would stare over or through my fingers at the stones that lay on those who were under the body of the church. Outside when everyone stood about after the service I would look at the grave by the door and then at the mounds lost in the churchyard. And I used to think how sad it was, not because they were dead, or because where they rested, but because of how little it mattered.

The church organ at St Edmund's used to be kept in life-breath by a pump activated by the swinging of a big wheel from which grew a handle. Two boys had to fling this thing backwards and forwards and I was one of them.

In Newport, in the corrugated iron church, the organ pump had been worth operating because it looked like a broad sword plunged into the side of the organ. With that you could always pretend you were King Richard or St George. But the pumping at Kingsbridge was only hard work.

On Christmas Eve I had been sent to bed as a punishment for creeping off to see the school play rugby. At ten o'clock I was roused, not by Santa, but by the superintendent, who said that all was forgiven and I had to pump the organ for the midnight service.

John was to be the other pusher. We wrapped up and went down the windy street and into the back of the church. All the people were there and there was that distinct, and rich, smell of alcohol in the pinching air.

Because I wasn't quite tall enough to catch the flying handle with any certainty I had to stand on a box. The carols started and there were we behind the scenes flinging the handle to each other and rocking the wheel at a good pace. Then we released it, let the wind indicator drop, and then started again. My hands were cold and once they slipped off the handle and I upset my balance and the rhythm of the operation. I managed to grab the handle as it came at me, but then tipped forward, off the box, just in time to catch the handle on its return. I caught it under my chin.

It handed me a punch like a heavyweight boxer wearing wooden gloves. Suddenly I was flying up among the Christmas angels. I landed with a sickening crunch and the last thing I heard before going out was the organ gasping for air most horribly at the pitching climax of 'Ding Dong Merrily on High.'

The mild winter went over its peak. There were days when we woke up in the warm dormitory and saw the windows streaming with cold, weary rain, and John and I would march the short crocodile of children down the running roads to the school.

Compared with what came after, we were in gentle comfort. The staff at the home were mostly young probationary children's nurses with bedtime-story pseudonyms like Auntie Nellie, Nannie, Auntie Judy and Nurse Sally. Three times a

35

week they were allowed to have their boy friends into the big room where there were accommodating chairs and couches and they used to have fevered necking sessions.

As we were permitted later hours than the other children, John and I would idle about while they fretted restlessly, and finally produced perhaps sixpence or a shilling to ensure that we cleared out.

By some irony it was while I was in the home that I discovered that I had a rich uncle. If not a rolling millionaire, Uncle Chris was comfortably off by most standards, with a car and a house in Barry, South Wales, and a business repairing and renovating ships that limped from the war into the Bristol Channel ports.

He was my father's younger brother and until he wrote to me after my mother's death I did not know he had existed. The protracted cold war which my mother had chosen to carry on with both her own and my father's family had kept him a stranger.

But when she knew that her life had only a little to go, she had reached out from her hospital bed and called for Chris Thomas and his wife Nance. With us so far from her she must have worried. She called them as the only people in the family who had any means or influence.

I can only believe that she wanted them to take us and give us a home. But it never happened. There were legal difficulties, she died before she could sign a paper, and anyway they were committed – both of them – to a business which occupied them fully and was essential to the war. But anyway they wrote often and they gave me some outside anchor.

In the woodwork class at school I had sawn and chiselled and glued together a tugboat with barges, and a steamroller which I painted red. These were my Christmas presents for Roy, my brother. He had to wait until February until he got them. Then he came from the hospital where he had been since the day after I had walked into that garden and knew that our mother had died.

I stayed home from school and waited for him from the

hospital. All his Christmas presents had been saved, quite apart from the toys I had made, and it was near his ninth birthday anyway.

He came into the big room thin and white as a stick. He sat down and opened the presents and then said: 'How's mum? I wrote but I didn't get any letters back? Is she better now?'

If I had been older and braver I might have told him then. But instead I just said: 'She's still ill. She's in hospital.'

'P'raps she'll be better soon,' he said. 'Then we can go 'ome. I didn't think we'd be away this long, did you?'

I felt hopeless and I said: 'We'll go soon,' and left it at that.

No one from the Homes ever got around to telling him. It was an accidental silence, I have no doubt, but it was bad for all that. It was only by some chance that during all the moving and the writing and documentation that followed, that someone did not drop the fact that we were orphans. It would not have been good for him to have found out like that.

As it was the Martins, the people who had lived in the terrace house that leaned on ours in Newport, had to tell him. It was when we had moved to London. He and I were separated and they were visiting London and went to see him at Woodford. They told him then. It was a year or more after she had died.

Now and again, at Kingsbridge and in the following years, I used to have dreams about her. Once I believed we were watching from the window of our old house and she was waving as she came up the street from the factory. Years later I dreamed she was sitting in the chair across the other side of the fireplace. I had our old cat on my lap and I was resting a book on him. And she was knitting and looking into the fire.

And when this happened I could feel myself happy in my dream and tell myself what a fool I had been all this time. Of course she was alive. Everything was back in its place as though somebody had been playing a trick on us. But then I would open my eyes and hear the breathing of the other boys and see the moon lying quietly across the beds. And then I would know what was true.

In the last few weeks at Kingsbridge, John and his younger brother George, who had no mother, were told that their father had been killed. Like mine he was a sailor, but in the Royal Navy. Young George had trembled with tears and I remember sitting near him by the big open fireplace. My mother's death I had kept a secret from everyone in case it should have got to my brother. But now I told George that I had no one either, as though my misfortune would help to lessen the sadness of his.

Late at night John and I had to go and lock the henhouse which was down by the paddock. We went down unspeaking that time, we locked them up clucking in the dark, and then came back again under the arms of the trees.

'I can't believe that it's happened,' he said at last. 'My dad. You wouldn't think that anyone would kill 'im. When the war was over he was going to get out of the Navy and have us with him. He promised.'

In March Roy and I went down the steep street for the last time, in our new suits and with the rest of our clothes in the blue bundles on our shoulders.

We went to London on the train. For me it was a prospect tingling with romance, a city of excitement and strangers. The sort of place where *things* happened. They met us at Paddington with an ambulance, presumably because Roy had been so recently ill.

As we skirted the streets I got my first view of the big town through the slit window of the ambulance. The midriffs of buildings, the greening tops of trees, half the message given out by the advertisement hoardings. I kept up an inadequate running commentary for Roy, who was lying on the bed. A woman sat there with us but, like so many of these travelling companions, she was neither communicative nor friendly. But she did point out the zoo as we went by.

Then, having seen the famous brick-wall poster, with the painted 'We Want Watney's' legend, I asked what it was. I thought it was a real wall; after all, this *was* London, the place where this cry for Watney, whoever he was, might mean revolution or anything.

'It's a beer,' said the woman in a tone so flat that no beer would ever be sold if it got to that. 'You won't want to know anything about it.'

We reached the Barnardo's 'Garden City' at Woodford Bridge, Essex. The ambulance stopped. I was told I had to get out. My brother was going to spend the night at the hospital and I was going to one of the small houses.

I hesitated. 'Come on,' said the woman. 'You'll be together tomorrow. Hurry up.'

I climbed out of the ambulance and I did not see him again for eighteen months.

4

PORKY, CHESTY, EAR'OLE, Israel, Darkie, Grandpa, Pongo, Rubberneck, Tiptoe, Ding-dong, Bug, Freddie-the-Fly, Professor, Snotty, Baggy and Scratcher Dan.

Depending on his habits, his proper name, his infirmities, his disposition, or his physical attributes, so each boy was nicknamed. Porky was a fat boy, Chesty a wheezer at night. Ear'ole had a mangled ear and Grandpa a hairy face. Israel was no anti-Semitic tag – the boy's surname was Hands and we had all read *Treasure Island*. Professor was studious, Pongo insanitary; Rubberneck had a mechanical movement of that joining part of his anatomy, so he moved like a tortoise, and Scratcher Dan just scratched. Breadcrumb, Bosky and Boz I have already listed.

The staff had names too. There were Korky, Chuck, Jessie and Rumbletum – and they were all women. Successive and oft-changing assistant masters were in the gallery as Marlow, Little Affie, Slinger and Walrus.

The day after I arrived at the Kingston home from Woodford I was nicknamed. They called me Monkey. I went into the dormitory on the second night and there was a reception committee sitting on the beds. They wouldn't let me go past so I stood, trembling inside, looking at them.

As boys go they looked villainous enough. Jerseys, blue and grey, patched all over, trousers embroidered in the same way, socks around ankles and bursting shoes.

' 'lo Monkey,' said one kid standing in my way.

'Trying to be funny?' I said.

'Yeah, Monkey,' he grinned. 'Let's see you swing on the beams.'

The others all laughed and I knew I was going to have to have a fight. 'What do they call you, then?' I said to the spokesman. 'Is it Ape? Or Chimp?'

He hit me on the side of the head with a sharp, stony fist. I thought he'd knocked my eye out of its socket. I went straight over the iron bedrail and landed in the hard valley between two beds. My head was screaming and I could hear them all roaring around and above me. I heard someone shrieking 'A fight! The new kid's 'aving a fight!' From the next dormitory came a deluge of booted onlookers.

I knew I'd have to get up and I knew just as certainly that he would put me on my back again. Having caught me with the sudden swing, he now pranced about at the end of the beds between which I lay, shadow boxing and yelling to me to rise and fight him. At that moment I couldn't even focus him too well, but I thought he was no bigger than me. It was just that he'd hit me first.

'Come on out, Monkey,' he yelled. 'Let's see your monkey face.'

My leg must have been sticking out because he got hold of it and pulled me out. They were leaping on the beds, and shouting and laughing. It was like being in a cave with them all calling down at me.

The fighter got hold of my foot again. My shoe came off and he staggered back against one of the beds. When he came back I was up to meet him. I never could fight. But I was bristling with tears and temper. I ran at him and felt the top of my head crunch his nose. He swore in short words. Now I was there I hit him with both fists, my bony elbows and caught him a cruel thrust with my pointed knee.

He was on the ground and I was on him, my angry fingers on his hair, banging his head against the ground. His nose was discharging like a red river. In the end they pulled me off and in the true manner of boys carried me away in noisy glory while they left him to bleed.

I might have won my fight but I had not gained my point. Even in the flush of victory they were calling: 'He's won! Monkey's won! Good old Monkey! Good old Monkey!'

Our dormitory was called Ruby Lord, after some earlier benefactor. Next door was Milne and the others were called Carless, Sutherland, McCall and MacDonald.

The entire building in plan was like a letter T, with the cross-piece and half the tail, three storeys high, and the remainder of the tail two storeys. At the junction of the strokes was the tower.

Once the building had housed orphan girls. They lived at the front and steamed in a laundry at the back all day. It had seen worse times.

Our dormitory was one of the two on the tailpiece. Underneath, down a cold back staircase, was a dark corridor, stone, with doors leading off to each side. We called this Death Row and that fitted it. The most important rooms here were the larder and the breadroom. No one I ever knew, not even among that talented and adventurous crew, had ever broken into the fastness of food, but the breadroom locks – plural because they kept changing them – could be frequently picked. And were.

In the breadroom for an hour each day was performed a sticky ritual called Spreading. Four boys, under the eye of a master who operated the cutting machine, spread margarine on inch-thick slabs of bread. It was established tradition that within reason the spreading boys could eat while they worked with their knives. Thus it was a favourite job, because you got only two slices for breakfast and another two – jam one day, margarine the next – for tea.

When someone had got the hang of the lock on the breadroom a raid would be mounted. While the thieves were down there, working on the door in the tunnel of darkness, there was a tense expectancy in the dormitory. Those left behind lay rigid and eyed the closed doors of the dormitory matrons' rooms which were on the landing outside. Then the slipping shadows of the raiders would filter back and they and their friends ate slices below the blankets.

A swing door away from the stone corridor was a cauldron of steam, spitting gas burners, and smells, that was the kitchen. There was a slab table, wounded and gashed by cleavers and knives, and a boiler with a grinning mouth which brewed the tea. If you went down there at night it was crawling with cockroaches.

A good Irishwoman called Mrs Macardle ruled the kitchen with a ladle and a spoon and a firm hand for the boys who helped her. She was a large woman, moving through the steam in a white overall like a ghost schooner appearing through the fog.

Occasionally a meek and wispy woman took over. She was an ethereal little lady, given to delving in the occult and communing with spirits. It was rumoured that she had been observed on the upper landing, robed in a dressing gown decorated with Zodiac signs, and singing incantations to the growing moon.

She was a sweet person, tweeting the choruses of hymns to herself as she went about her day. But she would not be put upon. She said so, and she demonstrated her determination.

On the other hand she was not a very good cook. One evening she had baked or brewed something mysterious for the staff, who smelt it briefly and decided it was uneatable. It was sent back in the hands of one of the boys. He returned later with the pudding and the message that Miss Clarry had said they had better eat it, or they would have to go without.

Another brief exchange of sentiments followed via the bewildered boy. Then one of the staff matrons seized the pudding and in a momentous and fiery temper stalked towards the kitchen. Miss Clarry, grey wisps of hair sticking to her pale sweated forehead, met her half-way. There was a clash of views, a swift passing of the pudding from one to the other, and then a brief entanglement at the conclusion of which the staff matron stood there petrified, with the pudding bowl on her head and the pudding rolling down over her face. There was wild and happy cheering from the unbelieving boys who watched.

On another occasion this formidable little woman of the steamy regions was asked if she would mind boiling out a pair of sturdy horns. They had once been the adornment of a highland ox, or something, and Mr Clarke, an assistant master with a love of scouting and the great outdoors, wanted the marrow boiled out of them. After that he proposed to mount them above his bedroom door.

The gentle lady responded and put the horns in a big pot over the gas. After a while they simmered and sizzled in the bubbling water. Then a strange, tangible aroma began to creep from them. A faintly coloured, smoky skein sneaked from the pot and spread stealthily through the kitchen. Miss Clarry was busily fussing when it stopped her in her eager tracks. Her

43

small nostrils trembled and she turned and looked at the big pot and horns on the stove.

Every minute the stench became fruitier and the evil mist more enveloping. The poor lady gasped and beat away at the thick air. Then, retiring to a corner, she removed one of her thick lisle stockings and returned to her duties with it tied around her nose and mouth like a bandit's mask. She was a game old dear.

Beyond the kitchen was the dining hall, a big tank of a room. Wooden tables and forms went down each side, there was sad linoleum on the floor, and green gloss paint climbed half-way up the walls where it met its inevitable brother yellow.

Meals were never elaborate affairs. Breakfast varied only between a sparse plate of cereal one day, plus a single slice of bread and marge and a cup of cocoa, to two slices of bread and dripping the next, with cocoa. On Sundays we had the boiled eggs. Occasionally at week-ends there was a slice of bacon, or ham known as 'walking ham' because it was rumoured to be high and active enough to escape if you failed to spear it quickly.

Lunches in the week we had at school, and it was just as well. Every day we returned to the certainty that tea would be either two slices of bread and margarine or two slices of bread and jam, and a mug of tea, with a rocky bun on Sundays. Tea was the final meal of the day.

I recall this with no particular vindictiveness, or any memory of having actually felt starving. But it is true. And after all, we weren't paying.

One morning I *do* remember, however. I recall it because the windows were starred with frost when we woke up. The fingers of a wind were feeling around all the corridors and we went into the same old breakfast of bread and dripping and cocoa. The cocoa was watery and hot, but so little sugar had been put into the cauldron that it was to all intents unsweetened.

We sat at the wooden tables, warming our hands around the cups and feeling the hot steam on our faces. The kid opposite me scratched a seeing-hole in the window pane.

44

''Ave a dekko out,' he said, peering through the space.

I scraped a hole in the window next to me and looked out. It was cold light now and coming across the yard was a thin boy called Thorn who waited on Matron in her house across the way. The yard was patched with ice and Thorn was going cautiously. His hands were around a large sweet jar, the sort you see on confectioners' shelves. It was full of white sugar. He was walking from the stores to where tubby little Matron was doubtless cosily awaiting her breakfast. She used to eat a lot of chocolates too. She had a very sweet tooth.

The house, The Cottage we used to call it, where she and the Gaffer lived, was a straight modern affair of red bricks, behind a tall hedge and standing in its own lawned garden. There were two trusted boys who worked over there before and after school, cleaning and washing up, and fetching and carrying from the kitchen.

We saw little of Matron in the main building, although occasionally she lumbered across the yard to look after the sick bay while the staff matron in charge of that department had a half-day. Every one of the staff held her in the deepest reverence and always stood when she came into a room, as we boys had to do. But she spent most of her time tucked in her sitting room writing letters by the dozen. I did not like her very much, but in fairness she was becoming elderly, just as the Gaffer was, and both he and she would have probably retired long before had it not been for the war.

They had a son, a handsome Army padre whom we saw occasionally, and who was married to a beautiful fair-headed woman. She was tall and completely dazzling. For a time they lived in a small lodge near the front gates of the home and I think they had a baby.

I remember I was digging in the garden, one Saturday, and she walked up the path. Her high heels tapped and she walked gracefully and her hair was smooth. She did not know many of the boys, and she certainly did not know me, but she smiled like an angel at me as I leaned for a moment on the spade. Never had I known a moment like that.

One of the ironies of Dickies was that although its shabbiness was without question, it had within it something grand and brave and displayable – the band.

This, until disillusionment, was the most thrilling thing for me. I thought that if I was lucky or played my cards right, I would be taught to blow the bagpipes or ring the cowbells, and, much more, blow or ring on tours and travels in every part of the country.

The band boys were the élite. They were older, they had different clothes, they got more pocket money, they journeyed to strange cities in a big van, and they lived in people's houses when they went. They had meals in *cafés*! They played in halls and people applauded them, and old dears snuffled into their handkerchiefs and felt for their purses.

It was a two-purpose outfit, this band. Arrayed stridently in kilts and jackets with flashing buttons, it sounded the fine and beautiful sounds of the pipe marches. Then came a quick-change act into page-boy suits for the indoor tintinnabulations with every variation of ringing and clanging instrument chiming in 'Bells Across The Meadow'.

The band returned from a tour in their van at the end of my first week at Dickies. They sat at their own special table (whether they had special band rations, I do not recall) and talked of what happened in Glasgow or Doncaster or the latest fabled and romantic place they had visited. They were expected to do no work about the place but to conserve themselves for the practice sessions held three times a week in their special room.

Certain boys, who looked as if they might be able to blow the pipes or make bells give music, were occasionally selected from the rest of us and ordered to attend the practices.

In the frantic hope that I might be one of the chosen potentials I used to wander whistling Scots airs through my teeth so that the Gaffer might hear. But he didn't, or if he did he never accepted the hint.

In my first month at Dickies it was decided to hold a church parade with everybody marching down to Kingston in their Sunday best with the band wailing at the front. They gave the band a trial march up and down the mudpatch we used for football and cricket. We all stood around the edge bursting with admiration and envy and a boy called Brice, who had arrived about the same time as me, came and stood at my side.

'That'll be me soon,' he said confidently.

'You – in the band?' I said, feeling the dark lump of jealousy and disappointment in my stomach.

'Going to start on the chanter next week,' he said. 'You've got to learn that first. Then you get on the pipes.'

'That'll be good,' I said, watching the band wheeling. 'Wish it was me.'

Even then my musical hopes, and my pride, were not finally damaged. That was to follow. As it turned out I was not even permitted to march behind the band in the parade.

Now, at this distance, I can think of it and know with certainty that nothing ever hurt me so much in my entire life as that refusal. The Gaffer had us all on the benches in the chapel, picking us out in fours for the marching column. He pointed to boys of matching sizes and each quartet went out into the playground to form up.

I was fairly tall, and I had reasonable expectations of being chosen for the first few ranks. But the Gaffer's thin finger stabbed around 'You, you, you, you,' and 'You, you, you, you,' and the icy realisation came that he had gone past my height group and was now picking the shorter boys.

Gradually, with each four leaving their forms, I went lower and lower in my seat, making urgent prayers that he would think I was shorter than I was.

But the room thinned and emptied, until I sat there with three or four other kids. Outside we could hear the pipes whining and warming up and the drums shuddering. The Gaffer stood up and went to the window. Then he turned and said briefly: 'Right, you go and get changed.'

I could hardly see my way out for tears. I went to the dormitory and got my working clothes on and looked out of the window at the splendid column curving around the playground with the pipes and drums setting the pace and the tune. The Gaffer, straight and proud like an old soldier, marched beside them with a stick.

Off they went, out of the main gate, and down Kingston Hill. I sat on my bed and thought of the marching, and the people full-faced at their windows and standing on the pavements. I wondered what I had done to be left out. I did not know then, and I still don't. Unless it was that the Gaffer thought I was too skinny to be a good advertisement.

Through generations of boys a slang had been evolved at Dickies, an insular language that left strangers mystified, and you had to learn from the start. Yet, strangely, the very word 'Dickies' had grown without anyone being able to recall or even guess its origin. It was just called Dickies and nobody knew why.

A boy was a kid or, more generally, a guy. Thus a boy from the home was a Dickie guy. Once a lad called Frank Knights, who went to a grammar school, wrote a letter to the London *Evening News* and signed it Dickie Guy and it was published with that name under it.

We used the verb 'to dig' meaning to appreciate, all-unknowing that it was a pet phrase of the jazz world, if, indeed, it was at that time. But there was a shade of difference; to us it meant to appreciate and acknowledge danger, like the 'cave' of the public schoolboy. 'Digs! The Boss!' meant the Gaffer was on the prowl.

A scoffer was a kid who ate everything he could get; a freezer was a shiverer in corners. A wildly cross-eyed kid was bosky, so was anything else that wasn't straight. A crook was just a crook, and a pot was a favourite with a member of the staff. Plonk was porridge, toppers were crusts, dush was money and tucks were sweets.

Saturday was dush and tuck day. There was a simple ritual. The Gaffer paid out the pocket money with one hand, then received it back with the other in return for sweets. It might seem harsh now, but it was logic to him, and to us too.

Strange it seems now, and stranger it must sound after what I have written, but in those first weeks, despite the small touches of misery, there came on me a feeling that I can only remember and describe as a sort of *settled* happiness.

Desolate though it was, with little enough for comfort and less for love, I realised that this was now my home and would

48

be until I was grown enough to go out and find myself some other place. Even during the months down at Kingsbridge, placid though they were beside what came after, I felt no real settlement, no sure contentment. This was because I knew they could not last; that some day I would have to go to some bigger and bleaker place. The countryside and the house and garden, the dogs and the pony, and the trees in the lane on the way to school, were only a young fool's paradise.

Also, during those months, there was talk and hope that Roy and I would eventually go back to South Wales to live with our uncle and aunt. But it did not come about. Now that both these things were taken away there was no more uncertainty.

This odd contentment at Dickies was not even a matter of making the best of things. After that very first pang of apprehension outside the gate, I never again felt afraid, nor continuously unhappy. There grew from this ugly old place, with its dripping rooms, its hollow dormitories, its riotous boys, a sense of warmth, of familiarity, of fun, of fellowship, that was strong and real.

There was a dramatic, unceasing stream of life flowing; a feeling of belonging, that grew up all unconsciously. On my first night in the iron bed in the three-rowed dormitory I promised myself that nothing was going to upset me here, I would allow nothing to hurt me, I would accept things for what they were and know that I could not change them. But some day I would walk out and start my own life.

My bed was my own, I told myself. My books were in my locker and they were my only possessions. There was a library downstairs and I would take the books and find some retreat and read and read, every day, and let it all go by me, until the day came for me to go. I would be an island.

This was the isolationist plan. But it never worked. You could not be alone in such a place. At least I could not. I was drawn into it and lived with it, reluctantly at first, but then to the full.

It was the boys who made it so. Being there was hard, or perhaps, a better word, robust. Outside, at school, the Dickie guys were the ruling tribe, defiant, warlike, rollicking, united by their bond, and ready for anything. Inside there was the constant adventure of keeping one move ahead of the Gaffer and all authority. It could never be dull. Difficult, but not dull.

If there was any resentment, it was the same one as I feel now after it is all long over. The hurt that simple thoughtlessness brings about. The thoughtlessness that made me have to lie to my brother because no one got around to telling him the truth about our mother. The same thoughtlessness that made them take us apart, and just forget we were brothers, without so much as a word of explanation from them, or a goodbye from us.

That was the worst of it by far.

5

ONE SHADED EVENING in the early summer, the Gaffer was sitting before us in the chapel. We always had five minutes there after tea to thank God for all the good things that had happened to us in the day. Quite often, after we had said the prayers and belted out 'Build On The Rock,' the Gaffer would sit saying nothing.

There was an unhappy vacuum of silence, we fretting to get out on the mudpatch to play dusty cricket, he inclined to have a peep at his paper first. He would wrinkle his nose over it, flicker his hooded eyelids at it, and occasionally say 'huh'.

Sometimes some item would hook his attention, some deserter getting his deserts, some thief with his liberty taken, some drunk banished to the jug, and he would read it aloud to us as a sort of extra lesson for the evening. He would, at times, become quite worked up about some trifling occurrence that merited only an inch or two of the paper's space.

He would read of the sentence on some crook in a voice black with warning, lick his lips around the words of the prison term and say with more conviction than any prosecutor: 'And serve him right too.'

His main racial discrimination was against Welshmen. If anything awful happened upon a Taffy he would relate it with relish. He frequently insinuated that as a race the Welsh were anti-Churchill and anti-Tory, and therefore rotten right through. This made it bad for me because I considered myself a Tory, and I liked Churchill, but I was Welsh.

On this particular May evening the Gaffer was investigating his paper when something drew him suddenly and he pecked at it like a bird spotting a morsel. He read it carefully twice and then said: 'Thirty bob each. That's not bad is it?'

There was a mumble of agreement that whatever they were, at thirty bob each they weren't bad.

It turned out that the bargain he had perceived was a pair of goats. It was the first act in the introduction to Dickies of the nastiest, most conniving, vicious, stealthy, sly, sinful, and stinking inmates it had ever known.

Three of us he sent to collect his goats. I've never worked it out yet why he wanted the wretches. Probably because he was intensely patriotic, he imagined that if they had kids (as if he didn't have enough) he would be able to raise a goat herd and thus help the national war effort.

There was Grandpa, a melancholy youth with spinneys of hair cropping his face, and Frank Knights and myself.

We claimed the goats from a piggery somewhere beyond the river and Kingston Bridge. The three of us saw the animals for the first time and knew we were buying trouble. One was fawn and white and the other white. Both had pink, sleazy eyes and sniggering expressions. I have never looked upon two more debauched creatures. Unfortunately for the Gaffer's ambitions they never got around to having kids. They were both billies.

'We oughta brought the cart,' said Grandpa, dolefully regarding the animals. 'We'll never get 'em back.'

The cart referred to was a sturdy hand-barrow which nominally belonged to the Kingston cleansing department and was supposed to be used by road-sweepers. The Gaffer had borrowed it years before and had never got around to giving it back.

'We'll walk 'em – like dogs,' said Frank, who was one of the brainy kids in the home. 'Let's get some string.'

The crook who sold us the goats gave us the string and looked as though he was tempted to charge us for it. We tied it around the stiff hair of their necks and set off on the return journey.

At first it seemed that it was going to be smelly but non-violent. The putrid pair trotted along willingly.

'It's going to be simple as anything,' I said.

'Yerse,' muttered Grandpa. 'They're too shagged out to cause any bovver. Look at 'em.'

The bother came immediately they saw a trolleybus. It was going at a spanking pace and the white goat tried to get underneath it. It pulled Frank with a swift and decisive tug. He gallantly held the string, but the goat was going to do battle with the low snout of the trolley, and nothing was going to stop him.

Fortunately the bus driver had good reflexes. He hit his brakes ferociously; the ungainly vehicle skidded and stopped. When it stopped the goat, horns down, vile glint in the eye, was three inches from death. Frank was only a fraction further away. The conductor of the bus had fallen from the platform on to the road.

There was huge confusion. Traffic squealing, bus driver in a near faint, conductor rubbing his backside, passers-by giving advice and trying to tug the goat away from the trolleybus. In the middle of it all the goat I was holding, and which had remained placid, had a hearty pee all over my boots. So interested was I in the animated scene that my first awareness of this disgusting act was when the warm water trickled through the lace-holes and soaked my socks.

I cried out in horror and Grandpa, who was tugging the string of the other goat with Frank, turned and shouted: 'Wot you standing there for? Come and 'elp us.'

'I can't,' I bellowed. 'The thing's just pissed all over my boots.'

A man who had been laughing on the pavement sat down on the kerb and began to howl into his crossed arms. Everybody started laughing and Frank's goat, with two little jerky frisks, escaped and galloped away in the direction of Kingston Bridge. A whooping posse followed it, with the elongated Frank galloping bonily in the lead. At the bridge the goat stopped and looked around mildly as if wondering who was causing all the confusion. Frank regained the string, Grandpa held it with him, and I splashed up with my goat which until that time had been more insanitary than violent.

But there was time. At the centre of the bridge my goat tried to jump the parapet. There was a small stack of concrete tank traps, the sort that were hurriedly moulded everywhere during the invasion threat. They were piled like steps on the pavement offering an ideal scamper for this goat who must have had mountain ancestors. The creature ended up straddl- ing the stone coping, forelegs over the river, hind legs over the pavement. In a red panic I released the string and grabbed two handfuls of the scrubby, stiff hairs on its back.

Frank and Grandpa, who were a few paces ahead, turned. 'It's trying to get into the river!' I cried.

'Let it,' said Grandpa stonily. 'Best place for the soddin' thing.'

Frank left Grandpa with the first goat and came to my aid. So did half a dozen passers by, several of whom had followed us from the last performance. A soldier got hold of the goat's tail and the animal began to bleat horribly. A gnome-like lady put down her shopping basket and began tweeting humane instructions, an action which she later regretted since immediately we got the goat down it put one of its back legs into her basket.

People on the river and along the bank below, accustomed to seeing human heads peeping over, did a double-take when they observed this one.

Eventually we got it back and having had its moment of glory it seemed satiated and content to be led along. So did the other goat, apart from an abrupt and momentarily terrifying charge at a nun, and we triumphantly led them into Dickies.

The advent of this pair began a reign of terror. The Gaffer had them set free at first in the fenced-off, grassy area beyond the mud patch. But he knew more about boys than goats. The following day one was discovered truculently challenging the traffic in the middle of Kingston Hill and was returned by a policeman who said it could have caused a messy accident and should be tethered.

So the Gaffer had the goats tethered. They apparently liked

their tethers because they ate them to the last strand and were next found pottering around the grounds of Kingston Hospital.

Chains were the next deterrent and they were more successful. But by industrious and secret tugging both animals were able to remove the stakes from the ground. Then they would break through, or go around, the fence and fly in fury across the mudpatch, over the playground, through the rooms and corridors scattering boys and staff.

'The goats are out!' the cry would ring. The Bulls of Pamplona caused no more scattering than this. Shrieks and shouts and tumblings. Down the Death Row passage they plunged once, with half a dozen boys just in front of their seeking horns and a hundred more shouting encouragement from behind. The pursued boys fled through the kitchen and gallant Mrs Mac tried to defend her territory with her ladle. But her bravery was brushed aside by the twin terrors who charged around and around the big table like tribal devils.

One of them – the white one – found a cloth in which some Dickies pudding had been steamed. It gobbled up the cloth and within the hour it was dead.

Boz, who had been on kitchen duties and had witnessed the entire drama, related it in the dormitory that night.

'After it 'et the puddin' cloth,' he said with relish, 'it laid down and sort of swelled up. We thought it was going to go off bang. Then it just conked out.'

'Fancy being killed by a Dickies' pudding cloth,' I remarked.

'It weren't the cloth,' said Boz scornfully. 'It was the bits of pudding that was sticking on it.'

The other goat lived for years. Its escapades continued after its partner's going, although it steered clear of the kitchen. In later years it became an embarrassment to a neighbour who would telephone and say: 'Your ruddy goat is in my outside lavatory again.' The goat one afternoon conscientiously trampled through every precious pane of his cucumber frame. He called and said something would have to be done. Mr Vernon Paul, who had by this time become superintendent, with a stroke of native genius offered to give the goat to the neighbour as a present. The offer was promptly accepted.

It was, of course, more a case of giving the neighbour to the goat. The animal continued and insisted on spending most of his time in Dickies grounds, with occasional forays into the neighbour's garden, who was powerless to do anything since it was his goat. Soon he moved house and left the goat.

The animal grazed and grunted at Dickies for all of fifteen years. It was a dun-coloured patch on the landscape of the home familiar to generations of boys. When it died, it had a good and peaceful passing.

The mudpatch, as hard and arid as a moon-desert in summer and veined with muddy rivers in winter, was our Wembley and our Lord's.

On its far fringe was a coastline of grass and weeds that was forever receding before the eroding mud. There was a boarded fence at the top cutting us off from the customers on Coombe Hill Golf Course and at that same end some knobbly trees that had dug their fingers underground and brought them up in distant places. These roots used to bend near the muddy surface like beartraps. They were a potent danger to visiting football teams who did not know them, and we nearly always forgot to mention it. Partly because of this, partly because our goalposts were home-made and to our own specifications, and partly because we could play soccer supremely well, we hardly ever lost a match.

Some boys spent their every free moment making intricate patterns across the mudpatch with a tennis ball at their toe. A studiously bespectacled boy called Woods spent intensive hours, hands splayed, poised delicately as a dancer, flicking a ball between the big trees and around the roots and in and out the goalposts. Two brothers, Big Bug, who had once had polio, and Little Bug, had an almost circus genius for juggling with a football. Nearly everybody played. After school, in summer, there would be pockets of rushing, darting footballers all over the mudpatch, and unperturbed in the middle of them a hefty game of cricket.

On the playground, an area of asphalt pitted with holes as

though some outsize mole had been busy, were a couple of traditional cricket pitches, their wickets painted on a wall.

Cricket was no genteel pastime. Pads were considered unnecessarily cissy and nobody had ever heard of batting gloves. And if you think there is nothing harder than a cricket ball just try playing with a billiard ball.

This billiard ball was in circulation for half a cricket season being pounded down on the asphalt by bowlers both enthusiastic and fiery. It split a lot of rude cricket bats and almost as many shins. It gave rise to a sort of stock repartee; the bowler, having struck the batsman on the lower part of the body would appeal for lbw, loudly crying 'How's that!'

And the batsman, rolling or creased in agony, would reply: 'Bloody painful.'

One day a boy called Squirts produced a golf ball and proceeded to turn on the fastest and most lethal spell of bowling ever seen at Dickies. He hit one kid in the ear and he retired to the sick-room. Then Stephenson, a lad who had a natural gift for any game, took hold of the bat and hit the golf ball higher than a golf ball has ever been struck before. It almost vanished from sight into the slow summer sky. Then it began to drop far away beyond the slopes of the trees – over on the Coombe Hill Golf Course. We rushed to the fence, bowler, batsman, fielders, took away one of the loose boards, and the line of searching faces peered through.

We saw the ball bouncing on a green in the middle distance. Then a golfer appeared, stopped, looked at the ball, glanced around him, stooped, picked it up, put it in his pocket, and sauntered away.

In later times we paraded a football team that took on every comparable side in the district and beat it. We wore the red and white shirts of Arsenal – it was falsely rumoured that Arsenal had given them to us and this gave us added terror – and we thought nothing of hammering in eight or ten goals in a match.

Competition for the places in this team was keen. There was a slight lad who had been playing cleverly in some of the evening kick-abouts and it was decided that he should play in the next game we had with an outside team. The kid was thrilled, then crushed when the Gaffer vetoed the selection.

'Why did he do it?' I asked the boy on the back stairs. I was the captain and I reckoned I had a right to know. 'Well,' he grumbled, 'he says I'm no good because I've only got one lung.'

'Have you?' I said, because this was news.

He nodded miserably. 'But it's daft 'im talking like that,' he said. 'I play every night, don' I? And it's me left lung that's missing and I was going to play on the right wing.'

It was scampering around after a tennis ball on the way to school, during the first few weeks that I was at Dickies, that resulted in my first experiencing the comparative comfort of the sick-room. I tripped, the pavement met me half-way, and a few seconds later I was regarding with somewhat sick interest a forearm that had taken on the shape of an inverted U.

They took me home. Korky Leigh, the sick matron, a fussy kindly little woman like a mother cat, put the arm in splints and procured for me the best and sweetest cup of tea I had tasted since the last one my mother had made.

I was lying, blankets over me, on the table in the entrance hall. The Gaffer came up and in his gruff voice asked me if I was trying to dodge school. I said I wasn't and he ordered two of the band boys, who were resting between tours, to get the cart round.

They wheeled the noisy green wagon, with Royal Borough of Kingston-on-Thames Cleansing Dept emblazoned on the side, to the door, and I was carefully loaded on it. It had, that morning, been used for moving the waste bins and it still had the occupational odour about it.

But I felt quite grand, reclining on my improvised stretcher, blankets robing me, and being borne on a creaking dustcart. We rolled down to the hospital with people looking and staring as though I were a wounded veteran.

I had fractured my arm, but they soon had it in plaster and back home I went and into the sick-bay. Korky thought it was best I should be there for a while 'to get over the shock' and I didn't mind.

The sick-room was warmer, more enclosed and homely,

than the other places. There were some bright pictures and some rugs. And there was a radio.

Not for eight months had I heard the radio and I saw it like an old friend. In the old days, when the winter was heavy outside, and the sky was full of wind, and the pavements cold and shiny underfoot, we used to cosset ourselves by the fire, mum and Roy and I, and listen to the radio from Children's Hour until bedtime.

The radio in the sick-room was on a shelf. In the afternoons Korky would switch it on and I would lie happy against the pillows and listen to the music and the talks about Genghis Khan and Chaucer and windmills and boats and fine deeds and battles and inventions.

Once, in the evening, the Gaffer stiffly walked in. He went to the window and gazed sternly over the playground. After some minutes of silence he looked at me, and then at my arm in plaster. 'Fooling about,' he said. 'No wonder you break your arms.'

I restrained myself from pointing out that it was only one arm. 'It's costing me a lot of money,' he lied. 'Two pounds every time they give you an X-ray. There's a fine thing. It'll take a lot of your pocket money to pay that.'

With that he stalked out. He never stopped my dush. He just liked to talk like that.

There came a day in that first summer when at last there was some fullness in the sun. It was a Sunday and even the early morning had the feel of velvet about it.

In the washhouse the water bounced in dazzling coldness into the enamel troughs. Boz came up to me, his mouth frothing pink with the toothpowder that came from the tin plate at the door. 'Swimming,' he whispered.

'When?' I asked.

''s afternoon. When she's finished. 'Ampton Court. In the Mole. Pass it on to Bricey and Breadcrumb when they get in'.

I passed it on. After breakfast the sun was swelled out, and hung like a challenge in the bursting sky. Stiff in our Sunday suits we marched to the cavern of the church, sat in the dreary gallery, and chanted the hour away. Marching back we saw boys heading for the river with their towels and swimming trunks. They were outsiders. Our swim would have to be an adventure in the art of smuggling and not getting caught.

In the chapel that afternoon Matron bumbled and mumbled, and I could see a bee in the ear of a flower by the windowsill. The sun was willing us to come out now. Would she never quit? She was on about nicknames. 'They are so wrong. We have our Christian names as Christians and we should guard them because God gave them to . . .'

'Monkey.'

'Yeah, Breadcrumb.'

''ow long is she goin' on?'

'Don't ask me.'

She talked her course and then panted like a peke out of the room. The Gaffer came in and three or four at a time prodded at us to go out for a walk.

At last the finger lit on me, and Boz, and Breadcrumb, then Bricey and a couple of the others. We strolled as sedately as monks to the front gate, hands behind backs, with the sun tormenting us at each pace. Outside the gate, behind the fence. Then we went off down the road like the Sioux after Custer.

It was about four miles to Hampton Court. We ran a hot mile, then plunged sweating and breathless aboard a trolley-bus as it whirred around a corner.

We whooped over Hampton Court Bridge, across the flat and green the other side, then slid down the bank to the little River Mole which there slips quiet and unnoticed to the side of the big Thames. It is a deep and languid river, with fish in its olive cellars and with shadowy weeds running and folding like the long hair of girls. There is a backwater with some boats and quiet jetties and little leaning bungalows on the grass.

Our swimming trunks were hidden under our shirts. We changed like madmen and then, without a thought, flung ourselves into the sweetness of the river. It was cold at first, but swimming in midstream, with the sun full and warm on your face or your back, it was good. We splashed the water silver and called to each other with our chins on the silk surface, and the breath of our shouts minutely ruffling it.

High up the big trees looked down like tall men. In some

places they bent over the river as though peering at the fastnesses and the fish. And the sun made petals where it touched.

'Monkey,' said Boz, swimming up close. 'Did you know nicknames ain't Christian?'

I gurgled in the river. 'Well what d'you reckon the Gaffer is?' I said.

6

EVEN WHEN YOU are only a boy, scraping your feet to school or guiding a tennis ball between the cracks and squares of a pavement on the way home, for an unexpected moment you can get mixed up with history.

There was a reluctant spring afternoon when the sun meekly shone on the clean brick walls of the gardens on Kingston Hill, and at the kerb was a car as jet and smooth and shiny as a rounded beetle. Bosky and Israel, and some of the other boys in their blue jerseys, were bunched at the side of the car. They were all chewing industriously, and talking and laughing with someone sitting in the back seat.

Many times I had seen this car, and others like it, on Kingston Hill. They slid out of the deep lane between the rhododendrons higher up the hill. Their passengers were always service officers, usually Americans, splendidly uniformed and wearing grim expressions.

I could not know then what was going on. But the pink and white cottage under the tunnelled lane had a name that was to become part of a famous story. It was called Telegraph Cottage. Its quiet walls saw the planning of D-Day.

The cars that rolled down the hill from Telegraph Cottage often stopped when their occupants spotted us. They knew us by our blue jerseys and I suppose talking to kids was a change for them.

The car that waited on that pale afternoon seemed to be special. Twenty yards in front three motor cyclists sat across their machines. Israel and Bosky sauntered down and asked if they could have a look at their guns.

The motor cyclists glanced around and a man sitting in the back of the big car waved his hand. Out came the revolvers.

I got to the long flank of the car and saw there were two men in the rear seat. One was in air force uniform, the other in smooth khaki with fingers of medal ribbons over his pocket. His hair was sparse and when he grinned it was like a banana.

I had seen him in the newspapers. He was a general called Eisenhower.

He was saying: 'Okay, this is the last pack. Who wants it?'

I had poked my head down to look into the window. He said: 'Here, son. You have the last one.' He gave me a packet of chewing gum and I thanked him. Then he said something to the driver, the engine murmured and the car slid away down the hill, with its roaring escort.

In the evening I was sitting on the hot-water pipes at the end of the dining hall. I was reading and I absently took the gum from my pocket. While I was fumbling with the packet, the Gaffer walked in, saw the gum, and pounced. He snapped the questions at me, as usual giving me no time to answer. He stopped my pocket money for a week and sent me to bed.

'I've told you boys time and again,' he snorted, 'that I won't have you talking to men – and especially American soldiers.'

In the empty hours of one night I lay sleepless in my bed in the corner of the dormitory and listened to the slow grind of an aeroplane. It was crystallised, like the sharp sound of a wasp imprisoned in something echoing. High above, a pin-point of sound in the huge and silent sky.

I listened idly, sliding my hands out of the bedclothes and stretching them up to the cool iron of the bedrail behind my head. The mounds that were the other boys breathed in un-dulating rows, someone stirred and turned and there was a boy snoring at the far end.

Abruptly the voice of the plane stopped. There were ten seconds or more of drifting silence. I lay unworried, but wondering why it should cut like that. Then, far away, but clear, came an explosion.

Flashes like wings of big white birds flew across the dormi-tory. Guns began to bite into the dark outside and behind their barrage the air-raid siren sounded. In the bed opposite little Tommy O'Connor, the smallest boy in the home, leapt up-right, yellow hair standing on end, and began frantically to feel for his glasses on the locker.

The other kids were tumbling out of the blankets, pulling on their boots and overcoats. Boz, who, once he was asleep was well asleep, half rolled and then shouted irritably: 'Shut the bleeding row, will you! Can't anybody get any kip!'

I pulled him out on to the floor and he woke up. Then I clattered down the back stone stairs with the rest, out into the crashing night, and down the hole in the ground to the air-raid shelters.

There had not been a serious air raid for months, and noth-ing since I had arrived at Dickies. The shelter was long and ghostly and hung with damp. But it was a good place to be. We heard another hoarse engine overhead, the same cut-out, the protracted, ominous silence, then, much nearer this time, the explosion.

All night the guns were thumping and we heard the strong, uninterrupted engines of our own hunting planes while we crouched in the damp and the dark.

The summer morning came early and the birds sang with delirious stupidity in the grey trees as we crawled out of our refuge. The first night of the flying-bombs, the sinister doodle-bugs, was over. But they returned quickly.

It was a Saturday, I believe, and the Gaffer wouldn't let anyone out of the place, although we wanted to go swimming. About three in the afternoon a wicked shadow swooped out of the clear sun. Like a bird it fell, but nobody could run before it swept across the tower, missing it by a wingtip, and then exploded on the golf course a hundred yards away.

I was in the dining hall and Marlow, the Gaffer's assistant master, was walking through. He glanced out of the window and saw the falling shadow.

'Down!' he cried out. 'Everybody down!'

There were about twenty kids there just then. I was quick. I bounced on the floor, under a table, just as the impact of the explosion came. One of the floorboards came up and smacked me in the face. The shudder shattered the windows, flung the doors open, and resurrected the dust of ages in a choking cloud from the floor.

The next bomb, that evening, landed in the hospital grounds down the hill. Marlow, whose real name was Mr Marshall, took the ever-useful dustman's cart and some of the senior boys, and marched down the road to patch up some of the hospital windows.

Every day the flying bombs fell. We lived like moles, rushing out to grab meals while we could. From our shelter, one of four dug around the grounds, we had to go down the Death Row stone passage, through the kitchen and into the dining hall. One evening there was a lull and the Gaffer trooped us into the chapel where we prayed, sang our hymns and choruses, and were nearly obliterated by yet another missile skimming the roof and crunching somewhere much too close.

When we had picked ourselves up, the Gaffer, looking shaken and old, ordered us to run for the shelters. We stormed through the dining hall, and the kitchen, and our boots echoed up Death Row. Suddenly Breadcrumb, who was a pace ahead of me, skidded to a stop, and grabbed my arm.

'Blimey,' he said. 'Look. They've gorn and forgotten the door.'

The food store was gaping. We looked at each other, and, discounting dangers immediately, flung ourselves through the door. We were in an Aladdin's cave of prunes, figs, eggs, sausages, condensed milk, sugar, butter and Lyons' fruit pies.

'Come on!' said Breadcrumb breathlessly. 'Don't ruddy well stand around.'

We loaded our pockets and our jerseys with good things, then fled up the passage, across the short run of yard, and tumbled down into the shelter just as another bomb shattered the air.

The bombs flew every day and night. The Gaffer, ancient and brave, used to come tearing across through the shrapnel and the hideous noises, his tin hat on the side of his head. He would fall down the entrance to the shelter and then, peering into the gloom, make sure we were all accounted for.

Then he would growl: 'If I catch anyone outside he'll be for it.'

Out he would go into the danger and run on his elderly legs to another shelter.

What a man this was. He was a hard old bastard, but he had his own ideas about duty and responsibility. At an age when he ought to have been down in Cornwall growing flowers or rhubarb, he had the lives of a hundred and fifty ragtag kids in his hands. He would have perished willingly, I know, rather than have had any harm come to the roughest, rowdiest young criminal under his care.

But he got shorter of temper, which was understandable. There was a break of a few hours in the raids on the second Sunday and he was shaving in the bathroom of his house. He had the window open and I was in his view, innocently hunting for a piece of string with which to repair a decrepit tennis racket which I had acquired.

'That boy!' He bawled from the window, his face half lathered. 'Come here.'

I trembled and went over. 'You're throwing stones,' he bellowed. A splodge of soap slid off his face and hit the ground in front of me like a summer snowball.

'I'm not, sir,' I protested.

'Don't argue with me,' he answered. 'Go over and stand in the hall. I'll be over to deal with you.'

I went over to the hall calling him all the mean old sods I could think of. The hall was the entrance hall where I had arrived and stood that first day. It was the traditional waiting place for punishment. That morning I was not there very long.

The siren called and some of the staff matrons trotted down in their overalls and stood by me against the green wall. This was the normal drill until an air raid got bad, although God knows why they stood there because the hall was directly under the tower. If anything had smitten that someone would have had a lot of digging.

For a while there was no action. One of the more genial women pointed to my tennis racket and said: 'Someone's getting ready for Wimbledon.'

The remark was followed by an explosion directly from hell. There was a wild fluttering of matrons, and simultaneously the chief matron herself flew fatly round the corner, clutching her tin hat above a face contorted with concern. Her rimless glasses were awry and she was panting like a bellows.

'Fly!' she cried. 'Fly! God be with us all!'

She was always somewhat Biblical and dramatic in her utterances. But another bang convinced us that, whatever the language, it was good sense. Everybody made for the Morrison shelter in the hall. This was one of those contrivances like a steel table, with stout, wire mesh sides, so that anyone inside looked like a zoo animal in transportation.

There was not much room in it. I found myself being pushed from behind, whether by someone who was trying to get me into the shelter, or someone who wanted to nudge me out of the way, I have never worked out. Whatever the reason, I didn't get in. There was a wild scrum of middle-aged women wedged under the hefty steel top, a galaxy of fat, thin, and hopeless knicker legs and thick stocking tops. I did not wait to dwell on the scene. The guns began to fire and I belted through the dining hall and up through the escape route to the shelter.

Within the next few days our situation became so exposed that there was nothing for it but to load us on to lorries and escape. Most of the boys found themselves living in two square and sturdy manor houses in the safe flats of Norfolk. But twenty of us had another adventure first.

We went, on our lorry, out of London, and north through

the small ways of Hertfordshire. Three miles from Hertford itself we were taken from the road and down through a distinguished drive edged with thick shrubs and fine plants in summer flower.

The place is called Goldings. Here in a massive and, to my recollection, distinctly elegant building Barnardo's have a school.

For a month we were in its strange, military sort of atmosphere, where everything was done to the blare of the bugle – everything, even praying.

On the first night, in the dormitory, with the last washy grey of evening pale at the windows, the bugle pealed.

'What's that for?' I asked stupidly as they all began to fall from the bunk-beds.

'That's G,' one boy said.

'What's G?'

'You 'ave to say your prayers,' he explained, getting to his knees.

I got off my bunk, which was one of the top ones, and prepared to offer up my supplication. All around boys were crouching, heads bent, and a low mumbling filled the big room . . .

'Two queens and two aces . . .'

'I've got a flush . . .'

'So when this geezer gets to the door the dame is stark naked see . . .'

'I reckon he's better in goal, any day . . .'

'I was tellin' 'im about that tart we saw in the flicks . . .'

Across, on the opposite side of the bunk to me, a ginger-haired kid was rolling snot into balls and firing it expertly with his thumb at someone kneeling behind me. Another boy bent pop-eyed over a paper-backed book.

Prayers finished with the sounding of another bugle and everyone got up off their knees and resumed their activities. I never discovered why this nightly interlude was called 'G'. It may have been the initial for God. He must have been well pleased.

Early in the morning the bugle roused us; it summoned us to meals (which were better than at Dickies); and to a strict parade, where the school captain, a handsome youth of about eighteen, would bray out commands in a foghorn tone.

Each day the other boys would be marched away to their workshops where they were initiated in the practical arts of printing, carpentry and other trades. But there was nothing for us to do. We joined a formless band of displaced persons collectively called 'spare boys.' Sometimes there was an hour or so of skivvying in the dining hall or kitchens to do, but for the rest of the day we were free.

We were turned out to grass, as it were, into a large sloping field, and called in when it was feeding time. Sometimes we played games, but the days spanned a lot of hours and were sometimes clear and warm. I used to stretch in the longer grass and look up through its green columns at the slanting sky and the falling clouds. There was not much to do, not much even to think about. I wondered sometimes, in those enclosed hours, where my brother had got to, and what my friends were doing in the dusty street back home.

There never seemed to be anything to read, so I used to slip back in the grass and think about things until I rolled off to sleep.

The head at Goldings was a little button of a man, who had strong religious feelings and a stronger arm with the cane.

'Christ,' I heard one boy say. 'He cracked it down so 'ard I thought my arse was going to come off.'

'What for did you get it?' said the boy on the opposite side of the bunk.

'Caught smoking in the dyke. I got six.'

'He prays before he canes you,' said the other boy. 'The last time I had it he told me to wait outside. He shut the door and I had a gander through the keyhole. And, d'you know what, he was down on 'is knees praying like mad. Then he came out and gave it to me. I reckon he was praying for strength.'

Nevertheless the head's geniality stretched to reading out odd, interesting paragraphs from the newspapers at breakfast time, and to granting a special half-day off when there was an especially grisly war film on in Hertford.

For me the great joy of this place was a shining swimming

pool down by the sports field. Every late afternoon we had a couple of hours in it. It used to get crowded when the others came from the workshops but for a while the 'spare boys' had it to themselves.

The irony of it was that although there was this luxury touch, there was not so much as a tap with water anywhere available at night in the main building itself. I was feverish one afternoon and I went to the sick-bay where I was told to go to bed in the dormitory. Whatever I had was something more than a chill because I heard the other boys shouting and scrambling that evening in the dormitory through a sticky red mist. It got dark, and quiet and cold, and I lay limp with sweat, and feeling my face like fire and my body throbbing.

Devils and demons screamed through my fitful sleep, drums thundered and screams threw me into terrified wakefulness. My tongue was filling my whole mouth and I would have given my arm for a drink.

Out on the landing, I knew, there was just a single lavatory. I couldn't remember seeing a tap anywhere. Shaking and sick I got out of bed and went looking for water. Down the shivering stairs, out into the open, to the washroom. In the full moonlight I could see they had the arms of a fat, final padlock clasping the doors together. God knows why. I couldn't get into the dining hall nor the kitchen for the same reason.

By this time I was stuttering with cold and wrestling with a crazy delirium. I stumbled up the stairs again and into the sleeping dormitory. I got into the bunk and soon I was in the nightmare hands of the hellmakers again. The sweat was channelling down my body and I could see and hear, tinkling and sweet, clear splashing streams in my dreams.

I woke up again, this time almost throttled by my tongue, and hoping wildly, and widely, that it would suddenly torrent rain outside the window so that I could put my hands out and get some water. Somehow I had to get a drink.

Down from the bunk I half rolled, half slipped. The boy in the lower bunk was deep and snoring. I touched him and woke him up. He had been friendly all along, but most of the others hadn't troubled with us because we were outsiders and they were a couple of years older and couldn't be bothered.

69

When he was rubbing his eyes I told him I was sick and I had to get some water.

'There ain't any,' he confirmed. 'Some kids bring up bottles of water at night. But there's none in here.'

I sat on the edge of his bed, my shaking, sweating, icy head in my hands. He thought for a moment. Then he said: 'There's only one way, mate. Go in the dyke, pull the chain, and get some in your hands.'

I went out, flushed the toilet, and caught a precious bowl of lovely dark water in my palms. I drank it luxuriously, then I let the cistern refill, pulled the chain, put my hands down the old, stained, brown pan, and caught some more. This was also good.

The next morning I vomited violently over my sheets and pyjamas. I worried about the sheets. The boy in the bottom bunk told me of a mysterious rendezvous which was kept each day by certain inmates.

After dressing I rolled up my sheets and pyjamas in a bundle and followed the directions through some passages unknown to me before. I arrived at the end of a stone corridor where there were four other boys, each with his small bundle of sheets. I did not know any of them. I stood there and waited too.

'Was you wet?' said one conversationally.

'Me?' I said.

'Yes, you. Did you wet the bed?'

'No, no,' I said hurriedly. ' 'Course not. I was sick.'

'I do every night,' he said, not without pride. 'Every bleedin' night I'm wet, I am. So is he.'

He pointed to a yellowy youth who was inspecting his own sheet with a kind of experienced, almost professional, assessment. 'Two nights last week, I was dry,' corrected this boy. 'But I've done it every night so far this week.'

The other two chimed in with their personal nocturnal scores, then a man came along and unlocked a door and the soggy procession dripped in. I was in the rear. There were sinks and taps and we did our laundry, afterwards hanging it on some hot pipes. Having done this I sank to my knees and then to the bleak stone floor. When I woke up they had got around to installing me in the sick-bay.

Our evacuation to Goldings proved to be a dubious move if its object was to avoid the danger of the flying bombs. Although there was no unremitting attack, as there had been at Kingston, the bombs did occasionally nose north, above London. One of them brought a frozen five minutes of terror such as we had never experienced in all the time at Dickies.

The air-raid shelters at Goldings had been allowed to deteriorate until they were beyond use. So we were all instructed in the oddest sequence of air-raid precautions that anyone could have concocted in the entire war.

When a flying bomb was sighted by a watchman who was stationed on the roof, he would warn everyone by setting off the fire alarms. Then, having been roused to face possible death you were instructed to *put your heads under your pillows*. This extraordinary drill was put into operation on the first night after its announcement.

The shrill of the fire alarm – a frightening sound in itself – speared our sleep and we all lay there, silent and afraid. We could clearly hear the bomb droning across the sky towards us. It coughed closer with every long-drawn second. Nobody had moved in the dormitory darkness until one boy jumped from his bunk and ran to the window. He took one look, said 'Christ Almighty' and dived back to the pillow which was supposed to be his shield.

It was very low now, snarling nastily, and the light from its comet tail glowed on and off through the window. When it was as close as it would ever be I put my head under the pillow and prayed strongly for a couple of minutes. The bomb went over and crashed somewhere in the country miles to the north.

7

SOMEWHERE ALONG THE way, I suppose, there comes to everyone a time when they realise and mark the things that to them are beautiful and good. This is not necessarily a gradual thing. It can take all your life, it is true, or it can take a few weeks or months.

With me it took only a late summer, an autumn and part of a winter. In that time, when I was thirteen, I discovered the things, or the beginnings of them, that I have always loved.

A boy's mind is a circus of excitements. It is full of heroes and villains, deeds and misdeeds; dreams in which he scores goals, or finds fame or treasure, or beautiful and adoring girls. He does not, not often anyway, look at a group of trees idling against the sky and find happiness in the way they are. Nor does he notice that some words have shape and colour, nor that music is more than sound, nor that stone and wood are eloquent and lovely.

The trees are things to climb, and the sky is just a place for the birds to fly, words are solid, dull things like blocks of wood in the pages of schoolbooks. Music is all right as long as there are rousing choruses to sing or a jaunty tune to whistle through your teeth. Stones are to throw or clamber upon, depending on their size, and wood is something to cut with your pocket knife.

But it comes. It can occur quite suddenly, like a conversion, as it did to me. I did not stop caring about the other things. I still played football and had fights and threw stones but I had a new awareness of things.

We had left Goldings after a month and gone to Narborough, a village in Norfolk. About half the boys from Kingston were already there in an obese and elderly house just outside the village, on the road to King's Lynn.

It was here that I came to know the things I loved.

Afternoons in winter when the light goes early; water in its wild state, and shadows on water; lanes and roads in summer, empty and dusty; voices calling across fields at night. And strong, sweet tea, and warm jerseys; wild animals who do not see you first; trees, any sort; old maps and books and letters, brown and full of secret things. Every clear morning; simple, beautiful words. Seagulls, big blackbirds and homecomings.

I used to list them. Not just in my head but in a book I kept. In it I would write too the things I had read which I wanted to remember, and anything which had happened to me which was strange, or happy, or of some consequence. It was not a diary, although I dated the entries. I kept it a secret and showed it to nobody. Just in case they thought I was nuts.

Narborough was quiet and thoughtful, lying on the flat of the Norfolk landscape. Its houses were small, unremarkable, wandering from the main road up through lanes and spinneys at the back. It had a fine flint church that glowed like a warm, glad lantern through its coloured windows on Sunday evenings late in the year.

There was a stately house, Narborough Hall, graceful as a ship, set in a park at one end of the village. Narborough House, where we lived, was at the other. We had a long lap of parkland running from the house to where the rural railway reluctantly reached Narborough and Pentney Station half a mile away.

The park had a collar of woods, thick and high around it. Woods running with animals and flapping with birds, where you could build a tree-house and no one would ever find it. Woods which smelled like a warm oven in summer and crackled frostily in winter. The park enclosed by them was shaggy with rough grass, patched with heather and speared here and there by solitary trees. There was no stretch level or smooth enough for a football pitch, so we played over the tufts and the molehills, the abrupt dips and rises. It was a combination of football and cross-country running, but it was good enough.

The first weeks there were full of hot days; days, it seems now, of an almost mythical boyhood summer. Clean high mornings over the trees, big skies, sun all the time until we were tired, and then the musty evenings.

There was not much work to do, and the Gaffer would

release us after breakfast and we used to run out across the grass in front of the house. Long mornings, I recall, stripped to the waist, lying in the grass and reading.

Marlow, on a return expedition to Kingston with a lorry, had gathered all the books he could lay hands upon and brought them to Narborough. My own books, my valued 'William' books, had been brought with them, and when I asked the Old Man if I could have them back as my personal possessions he refused on the grounds that I had probably stolen them in the first place anyhow.

But they were easy times, stretched out with old Bosky, who was a great reader too, despite being wildly cross-eyed, captured by school stories, Sherlock Holmes, Biggles and Ballantyne.

About mid-day one day, Bosky, lank on the grass, threw down *The Gorilla Hunters* and sighed; 'Blimey, that was a bleedin' good book.'

He looked up from behind his glasses, over the top of his own head, to see the frowning form of the Gaffer. The Gaffer had his green suit on because he had been to King's Lynn, and his hands were forced into his jacket pockets.

'What did you say?' he asked Bosky.

'What, sir?' replied the trembling Bosky.

'About the book.'

'The book? Oh, the book, sir. Yes, I did.'

'What?'

'I just said it was a good book.'

'You said another word.'

Bosky thought. 'Bleedin'?' he asked anxiously.

'Where did you learn that?' said the Gaffer.

'From the book,' shivered Bosky. 'It's in there.'

'Show me.'

Bosky panicked through the pages, but hopelessly. 'It says that the bloke had a terrible bleedin' arm,' he said lamely.

The Gaffer caught him full on the side of the ear and knocked his glasses somewhere around the back of his head. Bosky went howling into the house. The Gaffer picked up the book. Then he looked at me. 'What have you got?' he said. I showed him my book.

'What's it like?' he said.

'It's a jolly good book, sir,' I said carefully.

In the afternoons we went swimming. A wide lake was lying low behind the trees a couple of miles away and in the buzzing warmth around two o'clock Marlow would take a string of boys across the low fields. We went beside a river choked green with reeds, over stiles and through curtained paths. On most days we saw Old Tom, the village idiot, sneaking his way through the high grass, a small bunch of flowers clasped in his chiselled hands.

The greeting was always the same, 'Waarm today, Tam,' we would chant, one after the other, the observation rolling down the line.

'Waarm today,' Old Tom used to return, grinning with his gummy lips and pulling at the peak of his old flat cap.

A rumour spun around that he was a German spy, although nobody ever took it a step further to wonder what he was spying on in that guileless place. Then it was said that he was really a detective, or a counter-espionage agent. But he was none of these. He was a glad simpleton who shouted the Bible in dramatic tones while squatting in the outside lavatory of his little cottage. He sang with avid enthusiasm, and louder than anyone else, all the hymns in church on Sunday; morning and evening. He sang every hymn to the same tune, but he loved Jesus dearly. At the watchnight service on Christmas Eve I turned and saw him kneeling across the aisle with tears coursing down his ugly innocent face as he prayed.

When you first walked to the lake it was like going on an expedition through a closed and secret land, and emerging from the shielding trees to see the sudden spread of brittle water. The first afternoon I plunged through the scrub and the woods with the others who had been there before, the ferns and the brambles clutching us as we ran on. And then there it was. The lake. It extended to the far distance, to where the big trees looked small, and then its shining tail curled around a headland and hid itself.

We swam there every day, stark naked for no one ever walked that way, feeling the joy and the freedom of the gentle water,

75

diving down through the liquid shadows, racing along the churned surface.

Someone had left a boat by the bank. It was a clever boat made from a big aircraft fuel tank fitted with poles as out-riggers. I think it had been left there by airmen who had been moved to some other place.

Marlow ordered that only the boys who could swim a hundred yards or more could voyage out on the boat. I had taught myself a version of the crawl which began as a flurry of arms, legs and water, and ended twenty yards later at little short of panic. It was physically impossible for me to splash a yard further in this fashion, so I systematically set out to attain the unhurried breaststroke.

Every afternoon I set myself a mark and thrust out my hopeful arms. A yard at a time I got to it. Within a week I eased my way along the measured hundred yards under Mar-low's scrutiny and he said I had qualified to go on the next trip of the outrigger.

Four of us went. I remember pulling on the wooden paddle at the stern and feeling the tubby tank moving under me, away from the place where the others were swimming. We pushed it across the broad midriff of the lake. We were coated with sun, the sky curved over us and the trees made a fringe around it. There was a taciturn heron sitting, still and splendid, on an out-thrust branch, and the water with its lumps of wood and floating leaves slid by without commotion.

Marlow had been invalided out of the RAF and had re-turned to Dickies as the Gaffer's only assistant. He was a shortish, good-looking man, who had achieved the near-im-possible of being wholly popular with the boys and being strong enough to demand respect at the same time.

He could talk with you on equal terms, tell good yarns, and yet never be held in the contempt that familiarity so often in-duces. When he lost his temper it was best to clear out. Any-where.

There came a morning when Breadcrumb George sat up in bed and announced that it was his birthday. He was one of those who had never received a letter or a parcel from anyone

in all his life. But that day one of the kids stopped him and said: 'Breadcrumb, there's a parcel for you in the Gaffer's office.'

Breadcrumb whooped a foot into the air and tore around, crazily, almost incoherently happy, shouting 'Guess what – I've got a parcel! I've got a parcel!'

He couldn't make a guess about who had sent the gift. But it was there. Plenty of the boys had seen it. About lunchtime the parcel appeared on his bed. He went into the dormitory and it sat there waiting for him, like a reward for goodness, beautifully tied, stamped and addressed.

Almost dumb with wonder and happiness he picked it up and examined it. Then he tugged and tore away the string and pulled the paper apart. Out on to his bed and the floor shot an avalanche of breadcrumbs.

With the infinite cruelty that only children can inflict on other children the trick had been planned, the bait laid, and the trap sprung. Breadcrumb George sat there crying salt tears, with the crumbs all around him.

Marlow walked in. Breadcrumb was a tough character and he was no great friend of Marlow's. But the master realised what had been done in the time it took him to stride from the door. Never had he been so angry. He howled around, blistering to get his hands on the guilty boys. No one told, so he cancelled the swimming for that day. Then he told Breadcrumb to get cleaned up and in his best clothes, he collected money from everyone on the staff, bullying it out of half of them, and took Breadcrumb into King's Lynn.

Breadcrumb crept into the dormitory late that night. He had a parcel under his arm containing a real present. He put it down on his locker, undressed and got into bed.

'What was it like, Breadcrumb?' came a muted voice from half-way under a blanket.

'Went to the pictures,' announced Breadcrumb. 'Got a new pair of togger boots and my guts full of cream buns. It was all right.'

There was another kid called Fatty Patterson who was known as Patty Fatterson. He was a big, usually placid boy with a hare lip, and pushed around by everyone. Sometimes someone would go too far and with a sudden tornado of temper he would lash out powerfully in varying directions, smashing up a few chairs or some plates before his wrath was dissipated.

The explosions were always impressive and the kids used to

try and provoke them as frequently as possible. One day Marlow got in the path of one of them.

It was in the breadroom. Bread, margarine and knives flew as Patty flung himself into his fury. Marlow went after him and Patty ran from the house and shinned a tall poplar tree at the gate with superb and unsuspected agility.

He stopped half-way up, clasping the trunk like a koala bear. Marlow and fifty boys were down below.

'Come on down,' said Marlow.

'Not much,' said Patty. 'You'll fump me.'

'No one is going to thump you,' called Marlow. 'Just come down. You'll break your neck.'

'Leave me alone,' hollered Patty. 'I'm stayin' up.'

He was left. The afternoon gathered itself in and at tea time boys appeared at the dining-room window with fruit pies in their hands, then apples and oranges. Patty, who was an enthusiastic eater, looked down from his tree.

'More fruit pies,' someone called out of the window. There was a reluctant shuddering in the tree. Then the leaves were shaken more dramatically as Patty descended. Down he came, walked fearfully into the house, like a gunman going to a duel, and joined the queue in the dining room. Marlow was giving out the fruit pies. He looked at Patty, Patty looked at him, the pie was handed over and nothing more was said.

Some of us lost a week's pocket money in bets that Marlow would thump him.

Fruit pies would have been a fine treat in the former days, but now they, and other good things, appeared on the tables regularly. We also had sugar in our tea.

Whether the precipitated exit from Kingston had stirred the Gaffer and his conscience to the realisation that we deserved better in life than bread and jam, I do not know. But we got them.

The place was better too. It had been built as a house and that made the difference. The usual comparison between home and house, one warm the other cold, was reversed for us. Dickies was built as a *home*, an institution, and all the chosen luxuries in the world would never have made it a house. But here at Narborough we had a house, with rooms measured in feet instead of yards, with two or three windows to each room instead of ten, with fireplaces, homely mantelshelves and doors that opened and closed.

Although we had less than half the boys from Kingston at Narborough, some had to sleep in a squad of nissen huts that had been abandoned by one of the services and stood like black half-moons beneath the cloudy trees in the park.

At first I slept in the music room of the house, a high and elegant place with delicate oak panelling around the walls. There were about twenty of us there, sleeping royally, but before the cold weather arrived I was moved to one of the corrugated huts. This had its compensations because we were allowed to have roaring fires in the bellies of the iron stoves and in the dark and secret hours of the night you could cook things on their glowing tops.

After tea one evening the Gaffer told us that an Entertainer was coming to entertain. 'He's going to give you a good evening,' he growled, 'so there's trouble for anyone who plays up. Trouble.'

He said this in a manner which seemed to indicate that he was not entirely convinced of the words he was saying. This was because he had already seen Affie. An hour later we saw him too.

Affie. We called him that for ever. He was a young man with a plodding Norfolk accent, large rural boots, and dark hair plastered down over his scalp. He had a wart on his cheek which gave him a somewhat circus appearance. When we first saw him we really thought he was a clown and the wart was part of his make-up.

But Affie was a rustic evangelist. He had a glittering piano accordion, a black and silver antithesis of himself, and a humping great book called *The Complete Home Entertainer*. He came to amuse and instruct us, he hoped, and to inject here and there a crafty word about God. We would sing some sea-shanties or lusty and harmless old ditties, and then a chorus or two of the sort we normally offered up only on Sundays.

Affie would always end with a short prayer, but he cleverly

concealed his true mission by beginning with a simple con-
juring trick, which we always saw – and let him know we saw
– before it was half through, or some innocently funny rhyme
which he had culled from his bumper fun book.

From the opening night the audience appreciation was not
high. Affie occasionally got some entertaining problem from
his book which he should never have attempted, and he would
struggle hopelessly with it on a blackboard until he stood there
morose, withered and utterly defeated.

Boz or someone would mutter: 'Now he's buggered,' and
everyone would laugh.

The Gaffer sometimes poked a suspicious snout around the
door and simultaneously attentive silence, or sufficiently
amused and polite laughter, would occur. Then he would go
off to his dinner and Affie's purgatory would continue.

Sometimes this yeoman showman would dry up completely
of ideas, of puzzles, or jokes, or songs to sing. He would stand
there under the gaze of fifty or more hateful boys, savouring
every second of his discomfiture. Desperately he would cry
'Now who would loike to do a bit of a turn, eh?'

Stubbornly we would squat there staring at him. He would
flush red and the straps of his accordion would do their utmost
to throttle him. Then he would say: 'The lad that does us a
bit of a turn – sixpence to him!'

There would be a savage charge to the front. Chairs would
tumble and benches would spring on end, into the air like the
opening mouths of crocodiles. Three dozen boys would be at
the front trying to sing, or recite or tell jokes, to the remain-
ing two dozen. Affie would have a nightmare job trying to sort
out the claims of who was first, and who had the best talent to
offer anyway.

One day he picked on Israel. Had he known Israel at all he
would have shrunk away, but he didn't.

Israel, a short lad with a mobile face, was asked by Affie
what he intended to do for his act.

'Dunno yet,' said Israel. 'Can I 'ave the tanner first?'

Affie wasn't as rural as that. 'When you've done,' he said.
I am certain that when he projected himself to the front

Israel had no idea of what he could do to entertain. He glared at us, then Affie, and announced: 'I'm going to sing.'

No one had ever heard Israel give vent to any vocal feelings, and when he began he was very flat. But the song was interesting, and gained in interest as it went along, because we all knew what was coming, and we waited with pounding anticipation to see how Israel was going to get over his trouble.

The song went:

> *'My old man's a dustman,*
> *He wears a dustman's 'at,*
> *He killed ten farsand Germans,*
> *And what d'yer fink o' that?*
> *One laid 'ere, one laid there,*
> *One laid round the corner,*
> *One poor soul, wiv a bullet up 'is 'ole,*
> *Was cryin' out for water.'*

He was having a bad time. It was not so worrying that Affie was standing there, his face red and astonished. Israel could have surmounted that. But the Gaffer was lurking by the door, wearing his grimmest look. Israel had to go on. With the inevitability of a pilot of a crashing plane, staring as his doom comes at him, Israel sang:

> *'Water, water, water came at last,*
> *I don't want your water,*
> *So stick it UP YOUR ARSE.'*

Defiantly he flung out the last sentiment as though knowing that it was too late to go back now. When he stopped there was wild and ecstatic applause. The Old Man streaked down the gangway making for Israel like a rugby three-quarter. One of the big sash windows was open and Israel went through it like a steeplechaser.

Off he ran into the moonless summer night and we could hear him singing his song afar off. He stayed away for a week, sleeping in barns and hayricks. When he came back the Gaffer gave him a good hiding.

It was strange how all the time you never thought of the Gaffer and Matron being married. Tall and white, he was still the boss to all of us, to be watched, to be feared, to be circumnavigated.

She went on her normal tubby way, pottering about in her sitting room as though she was still at Kingston, with her cushions, her chocolates, her budgie, and her everlasting correspondence.

Then when we were chewing the now monotonous fruit pies at tea one evening, Matron stumbled in bumbling with excitement. She couldn't speak. She had a telegram crammed in her podgy hand and she gave it to the Gaffer. He squinted underneath his glasses, then fumbled to put his reading spectacles on. She was nudging him frantically so that he could hardly get them out of the case. Finally he did. He read the telegram and his face altered.

He was an upright-standing man and now he drew himself to attention. 'Silence!' he ordered. We were silent. 'I've just had a wire to say that Mr Desmond, my son, has won the Military Cross.' He glared around. 'For bravery,' he added somewhat unnecessarily.

Then everybody cheered madly and banged their mugs on the tables. Matron put her arm through the Old Man's, and he patted her wrist and grinned his wicked old grin while the tears ran touchingly down her Pickwick face.

I was glad for them both then.

8

BY SEPTEMBER the tractors and their sugarbeet wagons were creaking under the red trees down the road through the village. We would tumble over the tailboards and sit on the lumpy cargoes, cutting chunks from the sweet vegetables and crunching them like apples.

The lake had a golden fringe now, it reflected lonely flying birds, and it was too cold for swimming. The boat was drawn up on the little beach, patched with leaves, never to be sailed by us again. There were wriggles of smoke from the village

houses in the morning, and Old Tom walked around in a strange, elongated muffler.

So long, and fine, and happy had the summer been that we had all but forgotten the possibility of having to go to school again. The village children had been seen trooping up the road beyond Narborough Hall to a one-roomed school, where they were instructed by a sweet, dumpy lady with a crippled leg.

'we won't ever have to go to school,' said Johnny Brice when we were seeking conkers one afternoon. 'Stands to reason. There's no room for one thing. And there's no teachers. So we've got nothing to worry about.'

'P'raps they'll bring someone up from Kingston. Maybe we'll have lessons at home,' I said, letting my feet push through the leaves that hid the conkers. 'I wouldn't put that past them.'

I was half right. The next Sunday evening Verney Stephenson, one of the Dickies boys who was in the church choir, came flapping down the churchyard path as we reached the gate on our way in.

'She's 'ere,' he said, looking, in his cassock, like an angel bringing news. 'I got a dekko at 'er.'

'Who?' I said.

'Maggie,' he wailed. 'She's in church. You see. Sod it, that means we'll have to go to school.'

Maggie was angular and earnest. A dedicated woman who could be persuaded into the most gloriously fighting tempers if you kept at it long enough. She had been a teacher at our school at Kingston and, knowing in full the risks she ran, she had sturdily volunteered to travel to Norfolk to educate the exiles.

She was there in church, as Steevo had said, and she gave us a graveyard grin as we rose from our preliminary supplications. We could hear her droning away lustily through the hymns and psalms, providing rare competition for Old Tom who regarded her with solid interest.

After the service she patted as many of our heads as could not escape, and announced that she would be starting school almost immediately.

'Half will attend school in the morning,' she boomed brightly. 'And half in the afternoon. We shall be taking over part of the village school – they've been most kind, truly Christian – and I know we will get lots and lots of work done.'

As we walked towards home through the heavy dusk, I said to Breadcrumb, who had viewed the future with severe pessimism: 'Well, it's only half a day. Better than all day.'

'With 'er,' he said rudely. 'I'd just as soon 'ave no day at all. You wait and find out.'

I had no experience of Maggie's methods at Kingston because she taught a different class. But the stories of her provoked tantrums were now recalled and some of the kids began to look forward to school after all.

'She's got one word – what is it?' said Boz. 'She always uses it when she gets hairy.'

'Despicable,' said someone. 'She always uses it.'

'That's right,' confirmed Boz. 'She called me it so many times that I looked it up in the end. It means 'orrible.'

On the first morning we discovered Maggie enraptured by a shaggy and vacant bird's nest which had been hanging out of the hedgerow near the school for weeks. A bike, big as a bedstead, leaned against a bank of dying grass and autumn flowers.

'It's beautiful,' she was cooing, to no one in particular. 'See how intricate the little creatures have made their home. I *do* hope they hatched their family successfully.'

She beamed in her craggy way at the critical group of us who had gathered around her skirts. A new boy called Cabbagepants took the chain off her bicycle while we held her attention.

'We're going to have such fun, such wonderful fun,' she laughed as we started off towards the school together. 'Oh dear, the chain has come off. Never mind, we'll walk along together.

'We will really be able to study nature here,' she burbled. 'The changing seasons, the birds and the flowers and the first frosts. Oh, it will be such a happy, happy time!'

The old dear really talked like that. And the sad thing was she meant it. On that sweet autumn morning all the meanness and the hopelessness of the crammed, out-dated school at Kingston were no more, for her. She was ready for a new start. A clean, fresh effort, in the countryside she had probably pictured and longed for so many times in the yellowed classroom of a town school.

But the boys thought differently. Had she been a gorgeous

young thing with a soft face and a panting voice we would, no doubt, have followed her joyfully through the countryside, glorying in nature, and listened still and stunned in the class-room. But she was not. She said beautiful things, but she was not beautiful. Life so quickly became hell for her.

She laboured hard enough, putting crosswords on the board to keep us amused, traipsing through the fields and woods on nature rambles, on which we quickly vanished over the horizon leaving her breathless and distressed or just talking to herself.

The village school was one big room. For the purposes of our stay it had been divided down the middle with a thick curtain, the village children on one side and us on the other.

This barrier may have kept them from witnessing the appalling behaviour of the town boys, but it could not stop them hearing. A lesson would begin placidly enough on our side until a low rumble, like the stirrings of a revolt, would roll, then outbreaks of shouting and stamping of feet, then violent whistles, until poor Maggie was screaming to be heard over the riot.

The village teacher, the lady with the leg, would cry to her class: 'Out children!' and they would rise from their desks and hurry out from the place as though a time bomb or a plague had been discovered there. Every time we began the racket, so she would cry for immediate evacuation on the other side of the curtain. It meant, in the end, that the village children were spending all their time in the playground. They used to tell us to keep it up.

Maggie tried so pathetically hard to be fair and kind. We usually came in loaded with sugarbeet off the carts, slipped them under our desks and munched them throughout the lessons.

She was a bit shortsighted and she had not noticed this. But one day she spotted Boz chewing and opened his desk. Her face cracked into one of her patient, boys-will-be-boys smiles. 'How interesting,' she said. 'Now, does anyone know what this is?'

As we had been eating the root for a couple of weeks we knew quite well, but we led her on.

'A marrow, Miss.'

'A turnip.'

'A toadstool.'

'No, you're quite wrong,' she beamed, happy and grateful that she had at last caught our interest. 'No. It's called a sugarbeet. Now what do we know about the sugarbeet . . .?'

The poor old doll chattered on, and to add a little excitement to the lesson she announced: 'I'm going to cut this one up so you can each have a piece and taste it. Just see how sweet it is.'

Much to the chagrin of Boz she patiently segmented the sugarbeet, handing out a small disc to each of us. We chewed with exaggerated delight and enthusiasm. 'Yum, Yum,' we said, and 'Ain't it smashing!'

She probably never worked out how it was possible for us to go on chewing one small piece of sugarbeet throughout the whole day. She did not know that each of us, except Boz, had a whole root safely stored in his desk.

This sort of hilariously unpleasant thing happened every day, in two shifts, morning and afternoon. I was as bad as the rest. Once I was stood behind the blackboard for punishment and I poked the pegs holding the board out from behind, bit by bit, so that abruptly the blackboard descended on her foot. Everyone thought it was very funny.

Each morning she would bring one of us to the front of the class to read a passage from the Bible. She selected passages from each of the books, starting at Genesis, and we read one a day. Skilfully, and despite repeated requests from the class, she avoided the doubtful pieces in Leviticus and stories like Abishag the virgin Shunammite who was sent to see if there was any life in the dead David.

One November day, with the rain washing the school's small windows, Maggie called me out and gave me the open Bible to recite. I read it as we had always read it, gabblingly fast, the quicker the better, and get it over with. But only so far like that. . . .

Suddenly I knew what words were; that put together they sang like a song. I stumbled, then started again. But more slowly:

For, lo, the winter is past,
The rain is over and gone;
The flowers appear on the earth;
The time of the singing of birds is come,
And the voice of the turtle is heard in our land;
The fig tree putteth forth her green figs,
And the vines with the tender grape
Give a good smell.

When I got to the piece about 'the rain is over and gone' they all howled because it was teeming outside. But I did not look up at them. The words of Solomon's song made me ache inside and I was afraid it might show. I gave the Bible back to Maggie and, although she did not know it, and never knew it, she had taught her first and only lesson at Narborough. I knew about words, and I went on seeking them, discovering them, and wondering and delighting in their shape and beauty. For me Maggie had made a miracle.

At seven each evening the matrons used to sit around their big oval table for the evening meal. Miss Sauverin, dumpy and grey, for whom we had a name which I cannot recall, and Chuck, and Jesse and Korky, and the others, turned expectantly towards the door as we came in bearing the laden trays and steaming tureens.

I got the job just after we settled at Narborough. It was good employment because you received double pocket money, and you could eat anything that the staff had left over from their meal: two privileges not to be lightly scorned.

There were two of us, a powerful, quiet, fair-haired lad called Peter Lott who was given the job starting on the same night as I did. Curiously, although it was almost impossible to be thrown together with such a riot of boys without getting to know each one, I do not remember three sentences passing between us before that day.

Our duties were explained. We had to get up early, lay the staff breakfast table, serve them, get our own breakfast, and wash up before going to school. We did the same at lunchtime, taking turns, depending on what shift we were at school, and repeated the performance in the evening. We were also expected to keep the staff dining room swept, polished and dusted, and their cutlery and crockery in good order and repair. At Christmas we got five shillings apiece, and we gave the matrons a two-bob calendar.

On the first night Peter and I served the meal, whispering to ourselves the instructions on which side to put what and how to avoid pouring Brown Windsor soup down Korky's neck. Then, when they had finished we took the dishes to the scullery for washing up.

We were virtual strangers, and although we knew it was traditional for the staff boys to attack whatever was left over, we somehow hesitated from following it. We put the remnants of the meat pie in its crusty jacket on one side, and the potatoes and the beans. Then we filled the sink and began conscientiously to wash up. We were silent, dipping the plates in and out, and wiping them vigorously.

Eventually Peter said: 'D'you reckon this is going to be all right?'

'Yes,' I said. 'I 'spect so. More dush, anyway.'

'That's right,' he said.

There was a silence and we dealt with some more plates and dishes. Then he said: 'That pie looks good, don't it?'

'Have a bit,' I suggested cautiously, glancing over my shoulder to see if anyone was around.

'Might as well,' he said, grabbing a lump of brown meat and pale crust. He pushed the food into his mouth.

'Yes,' he said. 'Go on. You have some.'

I had a taste. It was getting cold, but it was delicious. We looked at each other once, at the door once, then like two swimmers at the start of a race, plunged in with both hands. The lot went, pie, potatoes and beans. We waited for the leavings of the pudding and had that too.

Then we finished washing up, full and satisfied with the night's achievements. We did the job for nearly a year after that, we became strong friends, and we never left a scrap in any dish.

These fringe benefits were well known to the other boys and sometimes they would creep through the dark to the scullery window in the hope of some benevolence on our part. Our friends we looked after.

Over in the nissen huts where I went to sleep they suggested, then demanded, that I should smuggle something over for one of the midnight fry-ups on the stove.

So one night I refrained from eating the leavings of a stew. Instead I stored it, thick and glutinous, in an empty cocoa tin, and concealed it until the time when I could creep over with it and heat it to edibility in the hut.

I loitered until I thought it would be a clear run. Then I took the tin from its hiding place in the staff dining-room cupboard and made for the door. I opened it and standing on the other side was the aproned Miss Sauverin, looking her most severe.

Sliding the tin around my back I stuck it up my jersey, balancing it delicately on the top rim of my trousers, where my belt pushed them out to make a little shelf.

'What's that?' she asked briskly.

'Where, miss?' I said, looking blankly around.

'The thing you have just slipped behind you?'

She used to spit a bit when she said her esses and the first syllable of 'slipped' caught me in the left eye.

'There's nothing, miss,' I answered, turning around and with some deftness sliding the tin around to the front of my jersey so it was still out of her view.

'It seems that you are taking something,' she said, scoring hits with the three esses.

I shook my head, turning around again and rolling the tin around my body.

'Concealing something!' she exclaimed, firing with both barrels this time. 'If you do not show me I shall get the superintendent.'

Knowing when I was beaten, I took the cocoa tin from under my jersey. She took it, opened it and peered in at the dead brown curd it contained.

'What is that?' she asked, not having seen moribund stew in a cocoa tin before.

'Stew,' I answered helpfully. 'Just stew. Saved from dinner.'

'What were you going to do with it?'

'Take it to the hut in case I came over hungry in the night. I often get peckish in the night, miss.'

She carried it like a bomb, or a rat, out to the waste bin and slopped it in. I watched morosely, thinking of the lads in the hut waiting to use it as a basis for their midnight feast. Finally she dropped the tin on top of the mess and said: 'I can't imagine how you could think of eating such filth.'

There was one hour of one afternoon of that winter at Narborough that I can almost touch even now. Its lines are as white and sharp as the spiky frosted grass was, as fine as the bones of the trees against the muddy sky.

It was about four o'clock. There was a hard, stony cold in the air and clamped on the land. Not a single push of wind came over the park and I walked across the iron lawns not going anywhere in particular, just towards the distance.

The tufts had frozen solid in the morning and stayed petrified all day. I did not have a coat, nor gloves. Just the blue woollen jersey that I always wore. I kicked at the white hedgehogs of grass as I went and then stole into a run over the rutted ground.

I felt very good. The coldness on my face melted as I ran farther and faster. There was no one around so I shouted, and some wood pigeons, which had been sitting cloaked and hunched like robbers in a tree, broke and curved away into the sky.

They were free and so was I. Free in a place filled with winter, with the air like ice, and the earth cowed and crouching. There had been hard grey sky all day, but as the sun was setting it escaped the clouds for a moment and the horizon was brushed with its crimson.

For a long time I ran, until my knees were red and aching and my breath smoked. At the end of the park I stopped and felt the perspiration crystallising on my face. There was a tree there, a good big tree that I had often climbed in summer. Naked now it stood alone on the grass.

I went up it easily, each hold and each place to catch your foot returning to mind readily as I went. Higher up some of the bark, brittle with frost, came away like a dead skin as I grasped the limb. But it was nothing, and I scaled to the shoulder of the tree without effort.

Then there came a difficult stretch, which I knew from the summer, but I scrambled and kicked and cut my shins on the trunk, until with no breath left in me, I made the top of the fine tree.

I stood there on its head almost, looking out on the groping afternoon, to the house with its yellow lights, to the last red stain of the sun in the other direction.

Of things done, and things remembered, that is the brightest of them all. The best of all good things is to be happy. And I was happy then.

9

ON THOSE DAYS the evenings came early, but advanced gently, like old horses wandering home across the fields. The classroom lamp was lit by three o'clock and by the time Maggie let us out it was fully dark. Sometimes across the park in front of Narborough Hall we would gallop, pretending we were riders in the night, and feeling the sting of excitement because we were trespassing.

Or sometimes down the road, and then into the village where the lights from the cottage rooms fell out across the bumpy pavement. The black-out had been ended and those lights were a temptation and, in one, an invitation. After all you were supposed to walk on the pavement, and it was narrow, and if you happened to turn your head and look straight into someone's warm and smoky burrow then it was not your fault.

If you hung about for a moment outside Old Tom's yellow window you would often see him at the wooden table, still capped and mufflered, staring ahead while his mother poured his evening soup. Then he would turn and see our faces grouped outside in the dark, and he would wave frantically with both arms, bounce up and down, and finally attack his soup with a demonstrative vigour that set us howling.

Then down the street, past the loitering trees by the churchyard, and on to some more houses and windows where we would peep, or goggle, until we lost interest or were chased away.

I used to love those hollow rooms. Their fires and their lamps and wooden tables the colour of cheese, their collapsed armchairs and crippled sofas, their indeterminate pictures on the wall and their great square box radios in one corner.

To me, on the outside, they seemed so cosy, so safe, that they might have been scooped out below ground, and the window through which I eavesdropped, a skylight set in the earth.

In one of the cottages lived the substantial Mrs Wright, her daughter Mary and their dog. It was an end cottage and the window did not face directly on to the pavement because there was a short path and a gate and fence of wooden pieces. Mary was a thin girl with big eyes and nearly black hair in ringlets. She had, like all the village girls, chosen herself a beau from the newly arrived Dickie boys far back in the history of the summer. Local consorts, faithful from early childhood, had been thrown over with typically female lack of ceremony once the new and robust Londoners came.

Mary's boy friend was Freddie the Fly, a minor leader in the Dickies hierarchy who had a small following and sharp fists. He would call at the cottage each day and walk with her to school, followed at a decent distance by his lieutenants and other members of his gang. The romance had more or less flourished throughout the idle summer and into the autumn and we, who had arrived at Narborough late when all the girls had been claimed or allocated, had to be content to watch with some envy.

For me the envy was keen because I liked the thin girl with the ringlets. One morning I recall attaching myself to the following of Freddie the Fly and waiting at the gate of her house while he went in and called for her. Out she came with her dog and her mum, and I said to Peter Lott, who was with me, but also not a member of the gang: 'I reckon old Freddie's got a real bargain there.'

Now there was a sort of solid wood handsomeness about

Peter, and as she came out of the gate that morning Mary took an interested look at him and turned shyly away, before turning back for a second look.

We went to school with Peter walking next to her and me next to Peter, and Freddie the Fly on the other flank untalked to and wondering what he had done to deserve this.

The drama quickened on the Sunday in church because Freddie was totally ignored and spent the hour praising God and kicking the front of his pew in temper. Peter was receiving a tide of warm smiles from Mary, and we both walked between the gravestones with her when the service was finished. By Monday the transfer was accomplished. Peter had a girl and Freddie the Fly did not.

'But really, I don't want her,' Peter said to me. 'Straight, I don't. I reckon I'm too young to bother about women.'

I was three months older. So I said, if it were all the same to him, I would have her.

'Right,' he agreed. 'You can have her. But you wash and I'll wipe for the rest of the week. All right?'

This was fair and reasonable, I considered, and as we had a wrestle every day I turned slyly, tripped him, and we rolled like a couple of mongrels over and over on the cold ground. When we were breathless we rested, and then he scribbled a note for delivery to Mary Wright saying, in effect, that he had decided that she was not for him, after all, and that his friend Les would be glad to deputise.

Freddie the Fly was now out of the contest, having withdrawn, in the end not too reluctantly, leaving the way clear for me. Now all that had to happen was for Mary to concur, which she did with no fuss, explaining that she liked the quiff which stood up in the front of my hair.

So I gained a girl, and not just a girl but her big bolstered mother, her idiot dog, a cottage, a chair, a radio and a fireside.

There was no difficulty in escaping to all of them each night. When the matrons had dined and disappeared, and the crocks were washed, wiped and stored, I would slide to the back of the house, through the lurking woods, walk along the shadow of some deserted stables, and out into the main road where she was never late.

There was always one self-conscious kiss, a cold little dab under the frowning wall. Then I would catch her hand, her dog would rustle from under some hedge, and we would run, all of us, to her cottage.

It was always the same. The gate whimpered, the latch sounded and the slice of light widened in the doorway. Then I was inside sitting in the formless armchair, soft and full of broken bones, with the fire at my feet and the radio at my ear.

'Well, what you always listenin' to that ol' thing for?' my

girl would say as she fidgeted and watched me. 'Music and talking. All the time.'

Her mother would come in, filling the room in one movement. She puffed and perspired like a bag of steaming laundry. She gave me cake and tea and asked me if I would like the radio turned off, and I always said no.

This was something good. Something I had almost forgotten, and I felt it warmly around me again with happiness and sadness, like putting on a familiar coat after a long time.

'Well then, what is on your hair?' said Mary on one of the first nights. She had a voice small like her face, with the Norfolk slur sealing in the end of each sentence.

'Lard,' I said, half listening to the wireless. 'Lard. I swipe it from the matrons' store cupboard.'

'It makes that bit in front stand up nice,' she observed, studying me closely. 'Have you got a middle name?'

'John,' I said. 'Just John.'

'Ahhhh,' she breathed as though she had chanced upon boundless knowledge. 'I likes that name. John. Yes it's better than your other. I'll call you Johnny.'

Thereafter she did. Occasionally when the mood fired her she would chalk on walls: 'Mary loves John Thomas,' and however ambiguous and ambitious this might now seem, there was no sophistication in that innocent and gentle place to interpret it in any other way than the one in which that village maid intended it.

She was a good girl and asked little. Each night, rain or bright moon, she would walk back with me up the road, our small figures silently together, and the dog going mad somewhere across the fields. When we came to the stables we would stop and I would kiss her again, warmer this time, but still only once. Then I would depart, I hoped mysteriously, through the trees, in truth keeping a fearful eye alert for escaped Italian prisoners of war, according to the Gaffer, were all over the place.

The romance went on unchangingly for a long time and when it eventually ended she wrote to me an appealing letter which began: 'Dear John, I've still got the same dog. . . .'

Every day Maggie, upright as an Indian chief, pedalled her high bicycle to the schoolhouse, no doubt telling herself that today would be better than yesterday, and inwardly knowing that it would, if anything, be worse.

The village children of that year were scarcely educated at all. The lady with the leg persisted in evacuating them at every mumble of a collecting outbreak from the other side of the big curtain. This was splendid in the summer and first autumn, and they reflected in their healthy faces the outdoor life they had come to lead. But the days changed and the wind flew swifter and colder across the open fields. The children turned blue, and jumped and stamped in the bleak playground trying to keep their little circulations running. Sometimes they pressed their icy noses to our windows to see if we had finished our rioting, only to turn away in disappointment, rasping on their hands and skipping sadly.

Maggie stood it superbly. It was a long time before she told the Gaffer what a pirate mob we were at school, and in the meantime she tried to inspire us to some interest in any legal activity.

Some of us she took to Norwich for a day. She was like a clucking hen, ushering us around the cathedral, the castle and the cattle market.

She showed us all the spired churches of the city from the cathedral hill, and the spidery flags of unremembered battles, hanging mummified in the dusty air over the choir stalls. It was a full day and we ate our cheese sandwiches and apples, and came home, well-behaved enough, on the train to Narborough and Pentney Station, in the middle evening.

The Gaffer made it known, on the following day, that there was to be an essay competition, judged by someone at Stepney, the head office, and with a grand first prize of five shillings. I wrote about the day at Norwich, called it 'An Exertion to Norwich,' and moved the Gaffer sufficiently for him to suggest that 'Excursion' might be a better word unless the outing had proved particularly tiring. I took his advice and changed the word. A week later I got the five-bob prize, my first ever earnings from putting words on paper.

Maggie announced, two days later, that she couldn't take any more. Bedlam was an everyday condition, but more she couldn't suffer. Water from the flower pots had been spilled on her feet, someone had stolen her spectacles, and she had a suspicion that half the class had disappeared while she couldn't see.

'Despicable! Despicable!' she moaned while the village kids clattered from their desks to the door. 'Oh, despicable!'

She submitted a list of names to the Gaffer and said she refused to try and control these louts any longer. Gaffer lined us up and walked along with the list in his hand. Each boy's name he checked and if it were on the paper he delivered that boy a resounding thump around the ear.

Twice he struck unfortunate innocent lads who happened to have identical names to real offenders. When he came to me I couldn't make up my mind whether to stiffen my neck muscles to take the blow, or relax them so that I rode some of the force.

He hit me while I was still thinking about it. I picked myself up and he said: 'You're a Welshman, aren't you.' It was a statement not a question and I nodded my head. He gave me another clump for being a Welshman. I stayed down this time, reasoning that it was pointless getting up if you were only going to be knocked down again.

In my pocket I clutched my precious five shillings prize money because I expected him to take it back there and then. But he didn't. Perhaps he had some hopes of me as a writer. But probably it didn't occur to him at the time.

After the autumn had fallen there was a pause while the fields waited for winter. They took on an empty look, dead and peaceful, and hardly anything moved in the still days.

The road out of Narborough went eastwards at one end and north at the other, but apart from the boys who had bunked and wandered beyond the immediate horizon, and excepting our one journey to Norwich, no one knew what was in the distant country.

One Saturday morning Boz was by his bed furtively shining his shoes on his counterpane. 'This place drives you mad,' he said with his everyday aggressiveness. 'Stark mad. Nothin' to do. Every blinkin' day.'

'Going to bunk?' I asked.

'Naw. But it's dead 'ere. Somewhere lively, I want, just for a bit. I'm goin' to Swaffham if he lets us out.'

'Swaffham?' I said, picturing the village road and where it crawled away to the nothingness. Swaffham was beyond that. All of five miles.

'Yeah,' he said. 'I've got two and ten. I'm goin' there. Want to come?'

'If he pays out I'll have about one and eight with the dush I've got saved,' I said. 'I'll come.'

The Gaffer did pay out and let us out too for the afternoon, mumbling his usual warning about keeping off people's property, and keeping our hands off people's property, which were two distinct and different things.

Boz and I went down the road to the bus stop, happy because we were free and off to a strange and exciting prospect. It was the first Saturday for a month that we had been allowed out, because, on top of the school crisis, someone had burgled the local pub and it was certainly a Dickie boy for no villager could ever have committed a cracking so expertly or silently.

But that day, or that afternoon, was ours. The air was damp and the sky hurried low, but we felt good because we were running for a bus, we had four and six between us and we were going to the bright lights.

It was a lonely road and the bus's tyres sizzled along its dampness. There was just one hump of a hill between us and the excitements and soon we were there.

Swaffham was a small disappointment. It was almost like Narborough's elder brother, touched with the same tiredness, the same oldness, although it did have some shops and a cinema. In ten minutes we had explored its interests, bought some apples, and wondered what to do next. Then we arrived outside the cinema, examined the posters and the stills, and recalculated our cash.

Boz nodded towards the door. 'Okay?' he asked.

'Okay,' I said, and we went into the cubicle of a foyer. Boz looked at the times of the films and his rosy face drooped. ' 's no good,' he said. 'Last bus back is at five, so we'll only see half the blinkin' picture.'

Morosely we went out. There seemed nothing to do but to wait for the bus back to Narborough, the next one, which was the same five o'clock, and the last.

'See if they'll let us in for half,' I suggested. 'We'll only see half the picture.'

Boz became businesslike and strutted to the paybox to put his cut-price proposition to the cashier. The discussion was depressingly short. He came back.

'Old cow,' he commented. 'Now what'll we do?'

Someone slipped from the darkness and, as they opened the door, we saw a cowboy on horseback wing a man with one shot of a rifle.

'Firing from 'is hip,' said Boz expertly, his eyes and nostrils wide as though he had smelled gunsmoke. 'Did you see?'

I had seen. 'Come on,' I said. 'We don't get 'ere every day.'

We marched to the paybox and thumped down our nine-pences. Boz said to the woman that he had money as good as anybody's.

'Pity you didn't show it first of all,' she sniffed. Boz blew a raspberry and we went in.

Inside, in the dark, we became lost in the picture. Mistily, somewhere in the thick air at the side of the hall, there was a clock glowing eerily, like a Hallowe'en pumpkin. We kept our eyes for the screen, but at the end of the cowboy picture we had to look at the time.

'Give it another ten minutes,' I said. 'Let's see the news.'

Ten minutes were gone.

'Another five,' said Boz. 'We'll run for the bus.'

Another five minutes. Then the second picture started. We kept glancing at the clock. Then, when the hands had gone so far that we knew the bus was already coughing its way towards Narborough, Boz said: 'We'll walk. Save some dush.'

We lolled back, like criminals or adventurers beyond the point of redemption or return. Now we were really in it. Now we could see the whole cowboy picture through again.

Five miles home we tramped and the rain went with us.

It dropped like chill pellets, eased off to a thick drizzle, and, when we got to Narborough, stopped altogether so that the moon could come out and have a look at us. Hands in soaking pockets, backs uselessly hunched, rivers running from our shoes, we journeyed without seeing a car or saying a sentence.

There was no concealment when we got back. We were briskly spotted, having already been missed, and sent to bed without tea, and the certainty of no pocket money for the next fortnight.

We lay in the solitary, shadowed dormitory, with our late companion the rain knocking on the window with an urgency that suggested that it wanted to come in out of the awful night.

'Good picture, Boz,' I whispered.

'Smashing,' he agreed.

Quiet then for a long time. Then I heard him stretch out his legs and arms and yawn.

'There's no doubt about it,' he said. 'When you're in a place like this dump you've got to get out and see a bit of life now and again.'

10

WHEN THE SNOW came that year it fell from the inside of a big, billowing storm that blew all of two days and one night. And when it was done the wind breathed over it all to make it smooth and presentable.

The storm was thrilling. Over the top of the woods the snow flew, sometimes horizontally, curving out and down like spume from a hurrying sea. I remember running face into it that night. Away from the house, splitting the crusted lawn and over the crackling park to the nissen huts, now like igloos and looking much better for it.

It was usually good sleeping in the huts because there were no matrons and no rules, or none recognised, and there were the fires that rumbled and reddened the iron stoves. But because of the presence of the stoves, and the absence of rules and matrons, there were nights when excitements became dangerous.

The night of the storm was one. The boys had been out lustily snowballing in the dark, and had run in late, soaked, and some of them only in their pyjamas. They were shouting and scuffling when I got in after finishing laying the next day's breakfast for the matrons.

I was like a sober man walking late into a party. Spikey Thorn, a reedy lad, was bounding from bed to bed trailing a flaming piece of sacking behind him. All the kids were jumping as he pranced around swishing the burning brand across the curved roof. The place was running with smoke and I stood abruptly inside the door as Spikey leaped down the line of beds towards me.

'Good ol' Monkey!' he called and swung the fire downwards towards me. I didn't duck in time and I felt the heat swell in my face. It went like a red curtain across my eyes and I jumped away, and ran out of the door into the snow.

Outside I realised it had not touched me. But I flew in through the door again in a temper hardly less burning than the thing which had caused it.

Spikey was standing at the far end, circling the fire around his head now. The others were still screaming and laughing at him. I pushed the nearest ones aside and ran down the centre of the hut. Before he could know that I was not joining in the game, I had grabbed the sacking from his hands and stamped out its flames on the concrete floor.

'You soddin' well burned my face with that, Thorn,' I said.

'Didn't touch you,' he answered from his stand on the bed.

'It did. I ought to know. You're mad you are.'

The boys had stopped to silence. Now they all began to jeer and shout 'Monkey, Monkey, poor old Monkey. Got 'is fur burnt. Ol' Spikey burnt 'is Monkey's tail.'

I reached up and gripped Thorn and pulled him down to me. Then I leant into him using both fists in my temper until I had hit him down to the ground. I was everybody's enemy then. They piled on me and levered me away. I blathered and screeched at them but they held me down.

Then because I was exhausted, they let me go. I sat up on

the floor and Thorn was standing a few yards away, holding his face where I had thumped him. A kid called Painter, who hadn't been in the home long, came over to me and said: ''Ow about fightin' me then, Monkey?'

'Any time,' I said.

'Tomorrer,' he suggested.

'Any time,' I repeated, noting that his eye was steady and feeling my outward sureness crumbling on the inside.

Everyone went to bed. Over the horizon of my blankets I could see the stove, still hot in the dark. I had a restless and convincing feeling that Painter would be a good fighter. We had a traditional system with fights at Dickies, a sort of league, where you knew your position and thought it your duty as a Dickie boy to keep or better it. The boys above you in the league you acknowledged as your betters as far as scrapping was concerned, although you may have never raised a fist with them. Those below you were your inferiors, or accepted as such, although likewise you may possibly have never met them in battle. The boy at the top of the league was usually the oldest, biggest and strongest, or most assured, and the boy at the bottom couldn't beat anybody and could only hope for the advent of someone smaller, weaker or more cowardly than he.

Spikey Thorn was a good many positions under me, but Painter was an unknown quantity. I reflected, with no calmness at all, that in the morning we would know exactly where we stood or fell.

The snow stopped when the first daylight came. We went over to the wash-houses, our towels draped like short capes over our vests, and the air was so cold it was stiff. I washed well away from Painter, but nobody had forgotten, and afterwards he was waiting at the plank bridge that went from the lawn to the park.

Word of a fight travelled swiftly and the encouragers were standing there too. I knew I would have to fight him, although I felt no more sure than I had in the night. I put my towel down and went towards him. We didn't say anything. We faced each other, circling symmetrically so that our feet fashioned a rough arena in the snow. Your breath always felt tight like a drum when you started in a fight and I could feel my heart banging against the drum now.

Painter looked and crouched as though he knew something about the game. He was shorter than me, but squarer and thicker and, I had a late suspicion, a good deal harder.

Shouted on by the boys, who wanted to see blood on the snow, we closed and jabbed the first blows. Mine caught him on the upper arm and he hit me surely on the left cheek with such crunching force that I knew then who would be the winner.

But the contest went a good distance. Once I thrust a lucky one to the side of his chin and he slipped and slid in the dip between the lawn and the park. He got out of the snow, ran over the plank bridge again and came at me like a small tiger.

I flew to stem him, but he was going at a good pace. His fists hit me everywhere at once, and abruptly I was looking up at him, and they were all proclaiming him the winner.

Suddenly everyone became aware that the Gaffer was watching. He walked over to Painter. 'That last one was a good one, son,' he growled approvingly. 'Right on the end of the chin. That's the way to do it.' He didn't even look at me.

Everyone went away cheering and I rubbed my bruises and reflected on the lack of justice in the world. After all I was on the side of right, I said.

The Gaffer might be admiring old Painter's killer punch, but he would have changed his ruddy tune if he had known why I was fighting in the first place.

Muttering, and quite alone, I began to walk away. Then something made me look round. Yes, it was there. My shape in the snow, thin but perfect, with each arm spread out beautifully, slightly raised, on each side of the body.

For a week the snow pillowed the banks, sheeted the fields and lay in blankets across the village roofs. Then the wind hushed, slowed, and the sun returned. The snow crawled away into rivers and streams and stealthily down the gutters and drains of Narborough's street.

The Royal Borough of Kingston-upon-Thames dustcart had been transported to Norfolk during the midsummer flight, and its foreign crest was by now an accustomed sight in the lanes and on the highways. After the snow had gone, the Gaffer told four of us to take the cart to the coal yard at Narborough Station, fill it with good nuts from one of the trucks and bring it back. We never understood whether this was a legal arrangement or a raid.

When we had done it he instructed us to scrub the cart and then trundle it five miles to Marham, where the rest of the

Kingston boys were living, carrying with us supplies for their larder, for they were getting low.

I was glad of the trip because there was a boy called Porky Blake at Marham who, since the spring, had owed me two shillings and I needed it. Grandpa, the hairy boy, Frank Knights, and the studious kid called Professor, who were more or less the permanent crew of the trek cart, were the others.

We took the lane that bent away south and then, creaking and grinding like an old field gun, the cart rolled along the wet road, still cold under our feet from the snow.

There were still white saddles of snow folded in some of the small places, and the hedges and trees were heavy with dripping crystals. We took it in turns to ride in the cart on top of the boxes and it went along metallically and at a fine rate.

Frank Knights was going to be an artist, and he squatted in the cart and sketched what he could see.

He nearly always had a sketch pad and he could pick out strange trees or clumps of cottages and draw them, just as I, by then, picked out words and tried to make things with them. Prof was good at all things except sport and he had brainy eyes behind his glasses. We all had some talent, some attribute it seemed. Grandpa had the longest hairs on his legs of anybody in Dickies, a fact which he boasted and I knew to be true because I was there when he was measuring them up against the other kids' hairs. He was also the first one in the home to be allowed to shave.

We reached Marham and gave them their groceries, and I got my two bob back because that week Porky had received a ten shilling postal order from his auntie.

Going back was easier. We had no load and two of us could ride the cart. It was getting on towards the finish of the afternoon and the sun, orange as it only is in winter, went down without great hurry like a man descending a ladder and feeling for each rung.

We returned when it was dark, and there was a letter on my bed from my uncle in Wales, with a folded pound in it as a Christmas present. The Gaffer usually opened letters and any money that was in them was kept for you, and you could draw it half a crown at a time. But he must have overlooked this one.

I pocketed it secretly and on the Saturday I went down to Narborough Station and got on the afternoon train to King's Lynn. The streets there were narrow and hurrying with Christmas people. It was very cold again and the wind sped around corners and whistled over the people's heads.

My intent, now I had money, was to buy Christmas presents; but I was standing looking in a bookshop window when it came to me, with some surprise, that I couldn't think of anyone to buy them for.

My brother there was, of course, but now I did not know where he was. My letters sent to him at Woodford Bridge had brought no response, and somehow you could not bring yourself to approach the Gaffer and demand to know where your brother was. For all I knew he was gone from me forever. It was Christmas, though, and I would have liked to send him something. For that matter I still had the half a tin of sweets which my elder brother Harold had sent, and afterwards kept his silence.

They were rightly Roy's, but he would not get them that Christmas.

There was a Christmas card for my uncle, and another for the Martin family, our neighbours in Newport. Then what? Then who? I remembered the superintendent of the home at Kingsbridge and his wife, and so I bought them a book in a little case. It had green binding and gold lettering, and it looked rightly sober and solid. It was, I remember, *Vanity Fair* and it set me back six shillings.

I bought myself some splendid banana gloves of imitation leather then I went for a walk down by the harbour. The salty gale was shrieking in from The Wash and the Lynn fishing boats were leaping convulsively like nervous ladies sitting on a series of pins.

The salt smelled good and it got on your lips in keen crusts. I had forgotten the smell. At Newport we had not been far from the sea, but the spice of it had fallen to earth under the pressure of smoke and soot and steam before it ever reached our street. But on the rare days when we had been on outings to Barry Island, we had stood on Cold Knapp or the Pebbs, as they called the pebble beach, and known the same smell and the same taste.

I remember one afternoon the old man came home breezily from sea and announced: 'We'll all go to the Empire tonight. And Barry tomorrow.' We went too. We sat in the gods at the Empire tasting every moment of the show and knowing that there was more delight to come the next day.

And at Barry Island we had paddled in water dyed with coal, and had a stick of rock each, and ices, and smelled that fine salt smell.

It was a winter taste that day at King's Lynn, though; although Barry had never been exactly tropical. It bit sharply and made my face sore, but I enjoyed the buffeting, the bending into the wind, and the thrill of seeing the bouncing boats. As far as I knew I was the first Dickie boy to come this far unescorted.

On the notice board, back at the station, I found there was an hour to wait for the train. The lights were on now and people shifted about like shadows behind the clouds made by their own breathing. I felt the cold getting through to me, and I stamped and puffed, and eventually went down to the waiting room where I discovered a big fire energetically jumping up the chimney.

I sat and waited for the short hour to go. The fire warmed me, I examined my banana gloves and decided they were superb, and I read the first two pages of *Vanity Fair* and wondered what the hell it was all about.

It was a frosty Christmas; set icy weather, echoing and crunchy, with nights when you could hear the cold creaking and groaning through the trees of the woods like a man walking in the dark.

We all went to an American Air Force base near Norwich on Christmas Day, and ate turkey, sweet potatoes, candied carrots and blueberry pie for dinner. There was a captain who told us to call him Shorty. He was six feet two and he took thirteen of the Dickie boys all around and showed us the aeroplanes, the ones on the tarmac, the ones in the hangars and two lying broken on the edge of the runway. I remember he took thirteen of us around because months later he turned up at the home at Kingston and took the same thirteen out to the pictures.

On New Year's Eve we were in our beds when a throaty plane came in low over the house. It was very near the trees; we could tell that because we could hear it swishing and we waited in the darkness to see what would happen. It exploded with a double bang and the next day we saw it up by the lake, all shattered, all dead and charred, and terrible, and with the body of the pilot still in a forked tree hanging out clear against the sky.

It was a bitter morning, and the lake was grey, like a happy person grown old and sullen. Our little boat had gone from the landing place. There were three of us and because we had been so carefree in this place in summer, and because of the aeroplane and the dead man, we went away sadly, but glad to go because we knew it would never be the same there again.

11

SOMETIME IN JANUARY the Gaffer got news that a great gang of Irish workmen had moved in and occupied his beloved Kingston Home. I was in the staff room when he came in seeking out Miss Sauverin, his grey old face moving like a river.

'See what they've done!' he cried, waving the letter in her face. 'See what happens when you turn your back! They send in the Irish. The Irish!'

Miss Sauverin wobbled, trying to get her glasses over her nose, and flustered at his agitation. She fastened the spectacles on and reached for the letter, but she grasped only air for by this time the Gaffer was pounding around the room like an aged and angry wolf.

'Irish they've put there!' he repeated as though someone was running a circus in St Paul's Cathedral. 'Repairing damage in the town! Well, we'll soon have them hoisted out. Out they will go! Get the boys ready, Miss Sauverin. We're going back.'

'Now, sir?' she shook.

'Now,' he shouted. 'The quicker we strike the better.'

It wasn't quite there and then. But within a couple of days the Dickie boys were leaving their exile. Down to the station came half the village, the vicar patting heads for the last time, the village girls, including Mary who still had her dog, all dripping tears.

The village boys were grinning and their school teacher, shocked with relief, stood like someone delivered of a dread illness. Old Tom, resplendent in his Christmas muffler and mittens, was there flowing with tears, and calling out God's blessing in a croaky voice like a man drowning.

At the other end of the journey, the Gaffer disembarked us and we formed up on the platform of Norbiton Station. Then he had the trek cart unloaded from the guard's van and ordered Grandpa and Frank to trundle it to the front.

Then we marched like a little army on Dickies, the cart our battle wagon, the Gaffer, cane under his arm, with that hoary old gleam in his eye, the inward light of every real warrior. We were wearing our navy jerseys and shorts and the Gaffer was in his green, hairy suit.

He halted us a hundred yards down the road from Dickies. We could see the yellow brick tower through the fanned branches in the garden of our neighbour Moscow Sam. The sight of the tower brought a new flush to the Old Man's gaunt cheek. He was the general, here were his troops. He was about to rush the enemy.

'Straighten up,' he said, cruising up and down like Wellington before Waterloo. 'Now – quick march.'

Off we went, the trek cart rolling like a cannon in front. You felt it was on the Gaffer's mind to order us to sing 'Marching Beneath the Banner' but he didn't, probably because it would have ruined the surprise.

We swung around the corner of the drive into the grounds of Dickies. Almost at once adjoining windows on the first floor were thrown up and two brick-faced, curly haired Micks poked their heads out and regarded us with interest.

'Halt!' bellowed the Gaffer right under the windows. We stopped with a crash and a shudder.

'Now there's a thing,' said one Irishman, looking across to the man in the other window.

'Sure,' replied the other, leaning on his elbows. 'There's a thing.'

The Gaffer, his face set like a pie, regarded them with the distaste he would have used on prisoners-of-war. Next to the Welsh he hated the Irish most.

It was the first Irishman who spoke again. ''Tis a foine bunch o' lads you have there, mister,' he said.

'A stirrin' sight to see,' agreed the other one.

The Gaffer said: 'We've come back. And we are coming in to take over.'

'That's good, mister,' said the first Mick agreeably. ''Tis a long time since I've had such bleedin' terrible digs. The quicker you're in, mister, and the little bleeders there, the quicker we'll be out.'

This rugged philosophy was ignored by the Gaffer, though it left most of us thrilled. The Old Man pushed open the front door, which to his surprise, and disappointment I suspect, was not locked. Then he marched us into the building in single file.

We stamped through the old familiar green and cream, the echoing places, like campaigners come home. The Gaffer discovered that the workmen were occupying the front dormitories of Dickies, so he compromised and established us in the back dormitories, threatening terrible punishment to anyone caught fraternising with the Irish.

On the first morning after our return I woke up in the seven o'clock winter dark and knew that there was a different and delightful smell on the raw air. I rolled over and saw that Boz had left his bed. Everyone else seemed to be under their blankets. I slid out and flipped on cold feet along the linoleum, following the summoning aroma.

Boz was crouched on the landing at the end of the next dormitory. I sidled to him. He gave me a startled look then grinned all over his ruby face.

'Diggy that lot,' he whispered. 'Go on. 'Ave a dekko.'

Stretching around the stair rail I craned down. The Irishmen were lining up before a steaming altar of sausages, bacon, eggs and fried potatoes. We watched with awful wonder as they filled their plates and went off, apparently not noticing the riches they carried under their noses.

After a few minutes the queue came to an end and the two white-aproned women who were serving stood back and wiped their brows.

'Tea luv?' asked one.

'Wouldn't mind,' said the other.

Boz, just in front of me, froze with joy, and I realised they must I .ve gone into the kitchen leaving their beautiful trays unattended. He did not need to say anything. We slipped down the stairs like a pair of hunting panthers. Two strides from the bottom of the stairs and we were at the loaded, sizzling trays, and helping ourselves like fury.

We grabbed something of everything, except the eggs, which were too slippery, then whirled and shot up the stairs and on to the landing again before anyone had caught so much as a shadow of us.

Boz was hopping about in a frenzy, which I took at first for excitement, until I realised that he had two scalding sausages dancing about inside his pyjama jacket.

He hooked them out and rubbed his burned stomach. 'Sod it all!' he cried. 'That was 'ot.' He slapped his belly to take away the sting, then we padded back to the dormitory with our loot.

There we hunched in the caves of our beds, while the light grew grey across the room, and we devoured our sausages, bacon, and fried potatoes, like winter squirrels gnawing into a secret feast of nuts.

We more or less finished at the same time, because I looked out and saw Boz's head emerge from his blankets in a small cloud of steam.

He grinned: 'You've got all fat over your gob, Monk.'

'So've you,' I said. 'You're all greasy. Did you get the sheets all mucked up?'

He investigated as closely as the grey light would allow, and
so did I.

'I think mine's all right,' I said. 'I put a comic down first.'

'Most of the grease is under the pillow,' said Boz. 'Nobody
will notice. What a bloody scoff, wasn't it? We'll do it again
tomorrow.'

At this moment Chuck's opening door beamed a warning and she came into the dormitory and switched on the lights. She used to stand by the door sipping her tea while we got dressed and made our beds. This morning her nose made some quick, small movements and we knew that she could smell the fried stuff.

Boz glanced at me and swiftly but quietly wiped his mouth on his pyjamas. I did the same. Chuck said: 'What's that smell?'

'What smell, Miss?' I said, sniffing ostentatiously and realising now just how powerful it was wandering about in the cold air of the dormitory, as hot and obvious as a chip shop on an iceberg.

'It's like cooking,' she said, staring hard and quizzically at Boz and then me.

'I know what it is, Miss,' I said with serene truth. 'It's the workmen's breakfasts.'

Chuck said: 'Oh yes, it must be.' And Boz looked over at me as though I were a mastermind.

Every morning we snaked off down the empty stairs and every morning we made our flying foray while Lil and Mare went for their tea. One day we had to be caught. We were.

'What are you up to?' said Lil, grabbing me by the arm. I wriggled and a sausage slid like a live thing out of the opening of my pyjama jacket on to the floor. Boz stood red in the face and red handed.

''Ere Mare,' said Lil, still holding me. 'Look at these two. Pinching all the stuff.'

Mare, who was mostly called that instead of Mary, emerged from the kitchen, her chin cupped in tea. 'What've they got then?' she asked.

Lil made us empty our sizzling prizes on to the table.

'You won't 'alf get it,' guggled Mare from her cup.

Boz did his Oliver Twist face and whimpered: 'We was 'ungry Miss. Starving. 'onest Miss. We don't get enough to eat in Dickies.'

'If you tell on us,' I said, taking the cue with alacrity, 'we'll be put on the slosh.'

Lil became pool-eyed. 'The slosh?' she whispered. 'What's that?'

'Bread and water,' said Boz. 'That's all we'll get. Don't leg on us, Miss.'

Mare half emerged from her tea cup and a sudden big tear slipped back into her tea. 'Bread and water,' she said. 'You poor kids. Give 'em some sausages, Lil. I don't see why those lazy Paddies should 'ave it all when our own kids are starving.'

'Nor me,' snuffled Lil, loading us up with food again. ''Ere take these and Gawd bless you.'

'Thank you, Miss,' we said together, making for the stairs.

'Come down again tomorrow,' said Lil. 'We'll see you get some.'

And so we did. And each cold dawn afterwards until the Irishmen went away. The other kids could never understand why every morning we used to give away our bread and dripping.

In the days after our return, the boys who were new to Dickies, the ones who had come into the home when we were at Narborough, went around hardly able to believe their ill-fortune. Neither the Germans nor the Irish had been able to change the place very much. True, it had less glass in its windows than any building of comparable size in Kingston, and some of the temporary occupants had written whimsical rhymes on the doors of the dykes, but these were small embellishments.

Nothing, it seemed, would ever be able to transform it from being a building of caves, tunnels, high echoes and cold comfort.

The yellow tower frowned from under its pointed hat; square, bleak and strong, as though defying any power to remove it.

The mudpatch was immediately ploughed by football boots after basking fallow for a whole summer and autumn. Some intrepid grass which had set out cautiously from the fringes towards the centre was soon routed. Everything was as it had been always. Mucky.

One day the Gaffer announced that some airmen who were going abroad had written to say they were sending all their sports equipment to us before they left. We watched for days, anticipating the railway van. It arrived, and two dozen hockey sticks were unloaded. But nothing else. All the rest had been stolen on the journey.

Dickies never had been much of a place for hockey, but the stoutness of the sticks seemed to have possibilities. We painted a cricket ball white and began a game immediately. It was wet on the mudpatch and the game, as pure hockey, was not a success.

Nevertheless a kid called Le Fevre, who everybody called Fever, chanced on the deft art of hooking the stick through an opponent's crutch.

'You rotten bugger, Fever,' said the injured lad. 'You'll rupture me.'

Fever laughed and the other kid smacked him over the head with his stick. In the following battle the ball was completely trodden into the mud and it quickly disappeared altogether as though glad to escape from what was happening. Both sides pitched in, whirling their crooked sticks. They were hooked around necks and legs, and between legs, and shattered over and above heads.

Some matron spotted the fight from her window and the Gaffer strode out, called us a lot of savages, and gathered the sticks saying that it was the last time they would be given out. It was too. The Gaffer always meant what he said.

Our sports gear always neared the primitive. Footballs were patiently patched and the punctures sought, found and remedied. Togger boots were precious, personal things, gained from all manner of places, guarded and never given up. We repaired our goalposts almost every week, for they frequently collapsed and the goalkeeper was often seriously stunned by a descent of the crossbar.

So when, one evening, the Gaffer brought Brother Bill, the Aussie sportsman, in to meet us, he was greeted as the greatest benefactor since Dr Barnardo himself.

He was going to buy new sports gear for Dickies. 'My name's Bill,' he announced loudly, 'and I'm from a place called

Sydney, Australia. I think you kids have been real sports when the bombing's been on, and I want to do something for you. Think of me as a big brother, kids.'

He laughed and the Gaffer came fairly near to beaming. Brother Bill asked him to select three boys to go out with him the following day to get all the new stuff. The Gaffer did and on the next afternoon, the trio went with Brother Bill down to Bentalls' store in Kingston.

They rode back in a taxi, an unheard-of delight, and loaded with footballs, boots, cricket bats, gloves, pads. Brother Bill told us how he had nearly been picked to play cricket for Australia just before the war. Out of season though it was he grasped a bat and squared himself in front of the wicket painted on the wall in the playground. Johnny Brice clean bowled him with three consecutive balls and we thought he didn't seem to have much idea of holding the bat. Not for a near-test cricketer anyway.

'He's rich as anything,' said one of the three who had been shopping with Brother Bill. 'He got all that sports stuff, and he bought himself a watch and a radio set and some other things. He's got millions, I bet.'

The Gaffer summoned us all to the chapel, where we had evening prayers, and we enthusiastically gave Brother Bill a special, extra mention following the Gaffer's dictation.

The Australian was red with embarrassment when we'd finished thanking God for him. He said he was only too glad to do something for such dinkum little sports.

The Gaffer ordered three cheers, and we echoed them willingly. Then we sang what we knew of Waltzing Matilda, and waved Brother Bill splendidly off in the second taxi to call at Dickies that day.

Three days later we got the bill. Not just the bill for the footballs and the cricket equipment, but for Brother Bill's expensive wrist watch, his radio set, and the other oddments he purchased.

Sadly we sent back the things we had not used. Bentalls told us quietly and kindly to keep the rest, and the Gaffer added Australians to the list of nationalities against which he was prejudiced.

Brother Bill was not much of a crook because he tried the same trick again somewhere else and got easily caught. He went to prison, but we did not think too badly of him because the thought of that night and the Gaffer praying for him was worth remembering.

12

THE WELL-REMEMBERED farmyard boots of Affie plodded into Dickies that spring. Affie was in them, and looking as lost as a country mole in a big city. He wore his brown jacket and his solid trousers, and his eye was as evangelical as ever.

He also brought his accordion, but as far as I recall neither squeezed nor squashed it in public during his few months' residence at the home.

Marlow had, sadly, gone away, transferred to another branch. Affie had written for a job and they took him.

He came out of Norfolk, with his square suitcase, and his ploughman's gait, to begin this new life. It never suited his gentle nature and ways, although he strove hard.

Every day he stumped around, greasy hair flung flat across his head and red of cheek, ordering boys to do things they never did, trying to get some authority in his shout but failing miserably as it skidded upwards into a piping shriek. More bread was stolen when he was in charge of spreading than had been appropriated in the entire history of Dickies, and he was often found, a lonely drudge in the wash-house scouring the sinks that were supposed to have been cleaned by boys.

About this time another master came to the home, an easy and able young man called Allcock, who was immediately and universally known as No-balls.

'I don't know why you don't get yourself a girl,' Allcock, who was in love, used to say to Affie. 'Do you the world of good.'

'Naw,' Affie would answer. 'Oim giving my loife to God.'

'Girls are part of life, and God,' the other master argued. 'Why don't you try and get fixed up? You'd like it.'

But Affie was not to be coaxed, and all the arguments and theories that Jesus was really in love with Mary Magdalene would not warm him to the idea.

In the end Allcock gave up trying to convert him and concentrated on his own girl.

One evening he took us to see a gymnastics display down in the town and she was there. We all thought she was beautiful. She sat right in the front row and crossed her legs. Breadcrumb George, who was one of the performers in the gym display, kept screwing his eyes around to see her. This was a pity because at one point he was supposed to be the key man in a human pyramid of white-vested enthusiasts. He was blinking at the young woman when he should have been correcting his balance, and the result was that the whole formation wavered and then cried and crashed in a pulsating heap, with Breadcrumb underneath.

Affie, who had fervour if little else, stuck joylessly, but bravely, to the task of identifying himself with our interests. He jogged out on to the mudpatch and brayed about like an old donkey while we played football. Armoured with his metal studded boots he charged the field from goal to goal and wing to wing, plunging about, kicking frantically, and, when he connected with the ball, usually sending it vertically into the sky.

With the same crusading enthusiasm and intention he joined in the games of British Bulldog which were battled out on some nights in the gym. There was nothing in the gym except floor. No equipment, no apparatus. It was merely called the gym to identify it.

Wild games were played in there on dark or rainy evenings. British Bulldog was a sort of infantry charge by one brigade of boys against another. When Affie joined in there was a tacit arrangement that at some stage both sides would suddenly stop piling on to each other and combine to pile on Affie. He would be ground to the wooden floor beneath an erupting volcano of boys. Bums, arms, legs all stuck from the mountain and more boys piled on the sides and on the top. Sometimes Affie's spreadeagled boots and fragile lower legs would protrude pathetically from the base, and as the news spread kids from all over the home would run to join in.

Eventually the boys would roll off, stunned from effort and laughter, and stagger back and stand waiting to see what Affie would be like. When the weight had all dispersed he would be left lying there, but he was bony and hard, and he would gradually get up into a sitting position and look around at us.

Then he would smile his good smile and say gently: 'Oi always seem to end up on the bottom don' oi?'

After some time Affie decided to go away to a religious settlement where he could train to serve Jesus. We were sorry when he went, but he sent us a nice picture of himself and some other young men wheeling a handcart along a road. A big notice on the side of the cart said: 'God Is Love.'

Affie was too, in a way.

Not long after Affie there came Walrus. He had a big, sad head, and a manner of standing, sometimes, with a face so blank that it looked as though the owner had gone away and left it.

He also had a tobacco moustache with damp ends and a pipe through which he sucked and blew alternately.

This was just after the war and he had left the army with a demob suit and malaria. Everybody knew about the suit because it aged before our eyes and was quite dead within a few weeks. But it was Israel Hands who discovered the malaria.

''Ere,' whispered Israel to a clutch of us in the playground one evening. 'Come and 'ave a dig at old Walrus. He's gone off 'is cradle.'

Eager for novelty, we followed him through the gym, up the back stairs to the bathroom landing. Israel hushed us and projected one eye around a corner.

'Cor,' he breathed, ''ave a dekko now.'

We did with a caution we forgot the moment we saw him. He was standing in the middle of the corridor, his wide face a waterfall of sweat, his steps like an elephant's on a dark night.

'Biscuits,' he cried out. 'Get the biscuits.'

'Wot's 'e want bleeding biscuits for?' asked Hands.

'Biscuits for the tank crews,' said Walrus as though answering the question. 'Biscuits for the men. Come on. Steady now.'

He made a lurch towards us and we went with avalanche

urgency down the stairs. The next thing we heard was that Walrus was in bed with malaria.

He was a serious and mild man, for all his size, and another one quite unsuited for the vocation he had taken. Apparently the Gaffer was one of a dying breed, for masters came and went with demoralising regularity. They strode in straight from the war, with a steady light in their eye, and staggered out, weeks, or sometimes days later, defeated utterly, and perhaps wondering if this was why they had fought the Germans.

Like most of them, Walrus attempted his best. Sometimes he would tell us about the thrilling battles he had seen, or about his family living in the Midlands, and how he missed them. But for me he contributed something special. He was the first person who ever told me that I ought to be a writer.

This happened three weeks after I had started a two-year course at the Technical College, the object of which was to turn me into something useful in the building trade.

Ever since the age of five, when I drew a ship hung with coloured flags and my mother had proclaimed me a genius, I had it in my head that I was destined to be a draughtsman.

'That's what you'll be,' mum used to say, apparently determined that at least one of her sons would not run away to sea. 'A draughtsman. It's a good job, and there's good money in it.'

I was at an age, when this advice was ladled on to me most regularly, when I imagined that a draughtsman was someone who poled a raft down a river, which sounded a reasonable occupation.

When eventually I discovered what a draughtsman was I still wanted to be one. The indoctrination had been good. Fever, who slept in the same dormitory at Dickies, had been similarly treated. He went around defiantly telling everybody that he was going to be an upholsterer because he wanted to work with horses.

The trouble was, my mother's ambition for me had never been matched by any progress on my part. When eventually I got to the Technical School I realised miserably that things are much better for a draughtsman if he can draw. I couldn't.

Three weeks after I started at the new school I caught chicken pox. The billiard room at Dickies was at last usefully occupied for there was no isolation room in the home. A bed was established in one corner and there, covered in scabs and boredom, I sat and wrote a story about an otter called Sleek.

Walrus came in to see how I was getting on. He read my story and said: 'You ought to have a go at being a writer, you did. Wait a minute and I'll go and get some books for you.'

He returned with the books which he said I ought to read if I was to be a writer. I read them all, and wrote frantically while the pox receded. When I got back to school I told one of the masters that I was going to be a writer and he said: 'Don't talk rubbish and get on with your bricklaying.'

But the inner thought, which had been lying there in the darkness from the day at Narborough School when I realised what words really were, had been given nourishment. Now, all the time, I was making stories, and reading, and telling all the Dickie boys that I was going to be a writer. The trouble was I did not know whether The Homes had any facilities for boys who said they wanted to be writers. Carpenters and plumbers were easily placed and if you showed any erudition or aptitude you generally got fixed up as a clerk when you left.

I did not even know whether the system *approved* of boys who wanted to become writers. In the night, in my bed, I used to wonder just how I would own up to it when the time came. Would they laugh at me and put me in a shipping office? Would I have the courage to tell them at all?

But so urgent was the want, and the desire to know what the reaction of authority would be, that I took a trembling chance and asked the Gaffer. He was warming up to one of his occasional bantering moods one Sunday while we were waiting for Matron to arrive and recite her weekly dirge. That week-end he had paid out the dush and distributed the sweets (which by this time were an extra, and no longer had to be purchased out of pocket money) without a murmur. Now was obviously the time to tell him outright what I wanted to be.

I was sitting on one of the benches at the back. I got up, gulped, marched down the lino centre, straight up to his chair, and announced bluntly: 'Sir, I want to be a writer.'

Slightly to my surprise he seemed unamazed and undismayed by the information, and after turning it over in his mind replied: 'Right son. Head office will fix that. And they'll see that you're a waiter in a good restaurant.'

Crushed and horrified I turned away and walked past all the grinning kids to my seat. Now, I reflected, I not only had the problem of becoming a writer, but the considerably more difficult one of *not* becoming a waiter.

Walrus, my mentor, left shortly after this, following what became known as the Pudding Incident. Occasionally, when there was anything left over from the day's meals, it was produced in the evening as supper. There was never enough to go around and it was, as always, the fittest and the fleetest who achieved most.

There were some suet-like puddings, round and heavy, left over one day, and Walrus bore them on a tray to the dining room at about eight in the evening.

He stood over them, like a master gunner presiding over a pile of cannon balls, and put up his hands to stem our involuntary charge.

'Stop!' he bellowed. 'First we will say grace.'

We halted, amazed, because religion had never been introduced into this particular routine before. Then Walrus clenched his eyes and ponderously thanked the Lord for arranging for the puddings to be left over from lunch.

It was not a long thanksgiving, but he took his time about it. Then he opened his eyes and saw that not a single pudding, nor a single boy, was left. On tiptoe we had advanced, and while he prayed we pinched the puddings from under the devout rising and falling of his wet moustache.

He went like a bull through the entire home trying to trace the puddings before they were devoured, but he never found a crumb.

Expressions like 'Godless villains,' and some stronger and of obvious military origin, tumbled from him. But he gave up for good in the end, packed his bag and went off to where the living was easier and more rewarding.

From most of the new breed of masters who came to

Dickies we learned something, and they learned from us too. That was why so many never stayed.

But some did remain and became part of our life, and we part of theirs. Their hopes and dreams and visions were dimmed like those of the others, but when they had buried them, they let them lie peacefully and just got on with living in Dickies.

One of those who stayed was Joe Errington. He could sing his way right through the songs of Gilbert and Sullivan in a profound baritone and mostly did. He was big and chesty, with horn-rimmed glasses and a stage laugh that was really his normal way of laughing. Liking him was infectious and within a couple of months of his arrival every kid from Tommy O'Conner, who was the smallest, to Frank Knights, who was the biggest, could sing blithely through a dozen choruses of any D'Oyly Carte production you would care to name.

Another one who stuck it was Jim Guertin, who had been a Barnardo boy himself. He had been a prisoner of the Germans and he was something of a hero figure to us all because, apart from being the best master at cricket and football we had ever known, he had lost a finger through frostbite when he was in a prison camp in Silesia. We used to gather around and stare solemnly at the stump where his finger had been and he used to tell us about the coal mines they had to work in, and how he and some others found a hidden gallery and used to play cards there all day.

One evening he took a few of us down to the river to swim. It had been hot all through the day and the sky and the ground still held the heat. The river was like a bale of silk unwinding. Thick and smooth and quickly it ran, like it always does when the water is warm. We swam for an hour or more until the river was darker and mistier, and running more into the sky every moment.

I remember this night because I swam on my back among the stumpy green islands in the middle and collided with one on which sat a regal swan. I paddled there, face upwards in the water, looking him straight in his black eye. He made a grating noise just as though he were sharpening something; I flipped over and swam like fury for the bank.

Jim Guertin was squatting there, looking vaguely in the direction in which the day had drained away.

'Sir,' I said dramatically. 'A swan nearly had me.'

'Hmm,' he said. 'What do you think of Miss Chalk?'

I looked at him hard and was about to go back to talking about the swan when I realised he wouldn't be interested.

'Miss Chalk?' I said. 'Well, she's all right.'

I had not given her a thought that night, but she was a small, pretty button of a girl, easily the youngest and most attractive of the matrons in Dickies. She had never had much to do with us because she looked after the very smallest boys.

Mr Guertin didn't say any more until we were on the bus and on our way up Kingston Hill.

'You think she's all right, then?' he said eventually.

'Who?'

'Miss Chalk.'

'Yes,' I said impatiently, while the other two or three who had been with us looked at him a bit strangely.

'That's what I thought,' he said. There was a silence, which was funny when you were with him because he was always talking. Then he said: 'You were lucky that swan didn't get you.'

Not long after he and Miss Chalk said they were going to get married, and they did too.

In the summer the mudpatch would bake as hard as old wood, fissured and grained, and swept by chocolate-coloured dust storms provoked by the summer wind. We played cricket on it every evening until the light went, pick-up matches with a lethal cork ball, and on Saturdays and special days, like Bank Holidays, proper matches.

One Saturday I was going in to bat, one ragged pad only and a bat that showed every promise of splitting before the afternoon was seen through, when Mr Pamelly, one of the ebb and flow masters about that time, called me.

'What are you doing?' he asked.

He was a fair, pink man with a small caterpillar moustache,

and he never played games. Still, I thought, he surely could see I was playing cricket.

'I'm going in to bat, sir,' I said.

'How long will you be?'

'Don't know, sir,' I said, slightly shocked that he didn't even know the rudiments of the game. 'Until they get me out.'

'Well, hurry up,' he said impatiently. 'You're coming down to listen to The Messiah.'

'Oh,' I said. 'What's that?'

'It's by Handel,' he said. 'It's about Christ.'

'Christ!' I said.

'Yes,' he replied evenly. 'About Christ. So get a move on.'

I limped in to bat, the top of the pad flapping like an old dog's tongue, because it was worn out.

'What did Pam want?' asked the kid who was keeping wicket.

'I've got to go and listen to something about Christ,' I said, taking guard.

'Smashin',' he said. 'Saturday too. That's a bloody liberty.'

Normally I used to get some runs, but that day the second ball carted my off stump some yards, and I turned and walked back.

'You didn't stop long,' said one of the fielders.

''Course he didn't,' said the kid behind the wicket. 'Poor old Monkey's got to go and see Christ.'

My side had to get somebody to field in my place, and I grumbled my way into my Sunday suit and followed Mr Pamelly and three or four other kids down into Kingston where a local choral society were doing The Messiah.

We sat in the gallery of the small church. Even now I can feel my chin hard on the dark wood, smell the dust of the church, and hear the gloriously rising sounds and feel the swelling of the exultation within me as they sang. Perhaps for a boy I was too easily moved, for it was only a nondescript choir and a church organ, but all I know is that it swept me away with its splendour and its joy, and I came out into the cool evening street knowing that again I had found something precious.

After that I listened to all the music I could. I was grabbing in the dark at it because I knew nothing of it, but had to go to everything I could. I walked to Twickenham one Sunday afternoon to hear Moura Lympany play at a hall, and sat frozen with disgrace and shame because not only did I applaud, or begin to anyway, between movements, but I did so during a quiet piece in the middle of a movement.

Then I walked to Wimbledon and queued and sat in the highest gods to see, or hear, for that was the important thing, 'Song of Norway' and the music of Grieg. I went to an amateur production of 'Lilac Time', and to see, again from the ninepenny gods, Rawicz and Landauer at Kingston Empire. These were patchwork choices, but I did not know what I was looking for and I had no guide. All I knew was that it was music.

By this time I was getting half a crown a week pocket money and I could afford these luxuries. I also got bus fares to my new school each day and, by running in the morning and walking in the evening, I saved that money too.

One evening I was returning from school when I saw a board nailed to the door of a house. It said simply 'Piano Teacher'. I walked on that day, and for many days after it, but I knew in the end I would have to go and find out how much you needed for lessons.

I did. I walked to the door and pulled at the old string of a reluctant bell. Whoever was inside seemed to have a painful job opening the door, and when it eventually swung inwards she was left coughing and gasping against the far wall of liquorice-coloured wallpaper.

She was a little woman, so untidy that I wondered right away how there was room for so much untidiness on one small person. She was dusty, fragile and old, and there was a funny, dank smell about the place.

'How much are the lessons?' I asked.

'One-and-six,' she said gummily. 'That's an hour and you buy your own music.'

My surprise and joy at finding instruction so reasonable must have shown. 'Have you got one-and-six now?' she said.

I had. 'All right then, come on in. We'll start. There's no time like the present, is there?'

I agreed there wasn't and followed her into what appeared to be a small cave, but was really her living room. There were books and piles of sheet music all over the place and a huge and ugly framed picture tugging to escape from the wall over the fireplace.

The piano, which occupied most of the room, held my eyes immediately. To call it a grand piano would be overstatement, but a good many years before it would have answered to the name. Its keyboard looked like a mouthful of bad teeth, chipped, yellow, and some missing altogether. There was a Guinness bottle squatting on the bass notes, and a lemon-coloured cat curled and asleep on the middle scales.

The lady laid hands on the cat. 'That's my Moggy,' she explained. 'He loves having a kip there, don't you Mog?' She pushed him and he flopped easily, lazily, over the lip of the keyboard like a pile of dough slipping from a pastry board. Then the lady removed the Guinness bottle, which was empty.

We sat down on the stool together, my piano teacher and I, and we began on the scales. Her fingers were stiff with rheumatics, fruity with lumps and knobs, brown with age and ancient with nicotine.

Her fingers met the keys and jolted back again like old people trying to do a dance. She was probably the worst piano player of her generation, and she would never have made a musician out of me if we had endeavoured together until I was as ancient as she was. But she was brave and conscientious and happy and we always liked each other.

In later lessons, in that old piled room with the afternoon sun squinting through the coated window, we achieved simple tunes, one called 'Merry Bells', and another, Rubinstein's 'Melody in F'. When demonstrating these she would bend herself bonily over the piano, summoning from it a sort of barrel-organ sound, followed not infrequently by the appearance of two, three or four beer bottles which rolled from under the instrument when she pressed a pedal with too much emphasis.

But having progressed so far we never made any more ground. I listened with delight still at concerts and tried to build my dreams by diligent attention to my scales, but at the end of many months and many one-and-sixes I still had only 'Merry Bells' and 'Melody in F' in my repertoire. Lesson after lesson I plonked through these two, and never anything else.

Perhaps I did not have it in me. Or perhaps the old lady did not know any more either. It's possible.

If the Gaffer had one fault, and he had more than one, it was that he sometimes let his old-fashioned imperialism loose on us, like a broadside from a Victorian gunboat, and tried to influence our political thinking.

It seems unlikely that a hundred and fifty boys, dedicated to the arts and crafts of living in a demanding place like Dickies, would have the time or sympathy for politics. But we did. More time and sympathy, I think, than those of our age outside because we were always together and we talked about things all the time. Sometimes it was God, and whether He smoked a pipe, sometimes about Arsenal or Grimsby Town, and, when the 1945 General Election came about, it was whether we were Labour or Conservative.

The Gaffer, after surely ambushing his conscience when it wasn't looking, told us all to be Conservatives. It was, he intimated, all for our own future good like believing in the Resurrection. Some day our faith would pay off.

He had a complete and permanent conviction that the English alone were fashioned by God, and that He had done his best work on the English Tories. The Scots he had to admit into associated membership because his pumpkin wife had her roots in Scotland, though heaven knows what she would have looked like in a kilt.

The Irish and the Welsh were treacherous parasite races, hanging on to England because it suited their situation, but ready to swing the knife at any moment. French, Dutch, Spaniards, and every other people, with the exception of the Ghurkas whom he admired, he regarded as coming a lap or two behind even the Welsh in the human race.

'We've saved the world again,' he would announce thunderously, out of nowhere, while we were sitting in the dining room or the chapel. 'Look at the red on the map and you'll see how we English have saved the world with our Empire. As long as we have men like Churchill born in England we will do it again and again.'

We remained unsurprised by these lectures, since we reasoned that he had to have something to jaw about sometimes. They were thrown up at intervals by something he had read in the paper, but when the election campaign was becoming intense we detected a quickening of pace and power on his part. Had we been old enough to vote he would, I am sure, have marched us to the polling station and personally checked that each of us had given his cross to Mr John Boyd-Carpenter, who was the Conservative candidate for Kingston-on-Thames.

This would have been from the best of motives, as were his lectures, since he was convinced that everything that had been sacrificed for the good of free men in five years of war, would be thrown down the drain at one moment if the election of a Government was simply left to the electorate.

'This Labour Party,' he would say with dire tone, 'is full of conscientious objectors. They wouldn't fight for the Empire. Ask to see their medals, and they couldn't show them to you.'

We would sit, five each side of the hard dining-room tables, our eyes on his cracked face, our chins on our fists, wondering when he was going to let us out, and he would continue: 'Churchill fought for the Empire. So did Eden. They've got the medals.'

He would be in spate like this for sometimes twenty minutes. 'How many of you have heard of Lord Beaverbrook?' he would suddenly begin. 'He's helped to build the Empire and make it what it is . . . and he built the aeroplanes that stopped the Nazis. . . .'

He would more than suggest that Lord Beaverbrook's Empire-building really won Canada for us and the school-master who gave the credit to Wolfe was a liar and probably a Communist. Some of his lectures were, naturally, lost on the smaller boys. Of three of them arguing in the gym after one session, two were convinced that the Gaffer was extolling the Kingston Empire, which they were not allowed to attend because it was too late and too lewd.

Sadly, the sum total of his propaganda campaign was that, by the time the election was due, every boy in Dickies was one hundred per cent Socialist. Someone cut out a big picture of Churchill, wrote 'Vote For Attlee' on it in crayon and stuck it on the wall of the Gaffer's private lavatory. The old man's conscience must have been shouting like a man in an empty room, because he never mentioned it nor did he attempt to sort out the rebel.

That August of 1945 I saw our house in Newport again. It seemed to have shrunk in the two years we had been away. Our blackened dog-rose clung sickly to the bricks at the front, weeds and rushy grass had covered the front garden. The entrance to the air-raid shelter still shouted outside the back door and the back garden remained like the surface of the moon.

I had gone to my uncle and aunt at Barry for a holiday and I returned sentimentally to Newport to see our street and our house again.

But there was no heartache in the meeting. I had gone away and had been taken into a different life so far and so fully that returning was only strange, not sad. Nothing much had changed; the holes in the front path had widened and some more of the gate was missing. But the number 39 was still on the top bar of the gate, screwed in with the wrong screws that my mother had used after we had detached it once and taken it away.

But it was not our house now. Unknown people were there, living in our cosy room, washing in our sink, shutting our door every night. I looked up at the window of my mother's bedroom where they had now hung green curtains. That last morning, when we heard her calling to us, she had been lying in that room, and had embraced us for the final time, and we had gone on to the landing stained with her tears and ours.

The people there now could not know of these things. Only that the family who had it before them had moved and the woman had died. It was nothing to them. They had their own lives and the past only belonged to that other family. And to the house, if houses remember.

All our friends were still in the street. Chubber and Flare and the other boys, and they asked me about Roy, but I could not answer them. But I was an outsider now, and glad of it in a way. It seemed that I had grown out of the feeling of the place, the environment, had journeyed and now lived in the great city of London. I had seen Waterloo Station and swum in the Thames.

Only once I did find myself running and calling with the old feeling inside of me. Being like I was before. I was staying with the Martin family, our neighbours in Newport, and one night, at midnight, I jumped awake and the whole town with me. Through the open window I could hear people shouting across the road and suddenly the air-raid siren at the bottom of the street began to whirl. The war with Japan, all that was left of the big war, was finished.

All the people were out in the warm night, standing at their gates and drinking beer, just as they used to do during the air raids. Under the lamp on the opposite pavement a man was swishing an accordion and playing 'The White Cliffs of Dover'. Some people were crying, but most of them were laughing and they began to dance around the lamp-post and the man who was playing.

The young boys began to run wild, in gangs, and suddenly I was with them again like we used to be in the old days. They built a terrifying fire in the middle of the road and went foraging for anything that would burn upon it.

We ran down the alleyway, behind the shops on the Cardiff Road, and began taking the big wooden gates and doors off their hinges and transporting them to the celebration bonfire. I was with the boys now, completely with them in the thrill and the spirit of the thing, feeling at one with their excitement and their daring.

There were roaring, roaming nights like this once, I remembered. Dark nights when we were shadows, fighting, throwing stones, whooping lawlessly as we charged like Goths.

Now I was with them again. Knowing the searing compulsion of being with a gang and running with its shouting tide. The shopkeepers on the Cardiff Road screamed at us from their windows and I recognised the greengrocer, nightshirted now, who used to say my whistling through my teeth drove him mad. They were unhitching his gate and he was shouting at them, and it sounded funny because he hadn't put his teeth in.

I jumped in to help, laughing like an outlaw, and bore the gate up the alley to the pyre that was burning the tar off the road.

My cousin was called Adrian, he was two years and a bit older than me and he could drive the car, and he had a girl who wore a flower in her hair. We went into a rosy café in Cardiff, when I started my holiday with the strangers who were my relatives, and the girl was sitting there with some other young people.

I thought she was beautiful, but Adrian treated her casually because he obviously had lots of other women, and on this day he promised he would take her for a drive in the evening if he could find the time.

I was aghast that he should treat her so idly. Fancy having *her* driving along with you in a car – *at night*! But he was a man of the world, and I could only watch a little segment of his life and feel a bit jealous that this could not have been my life too.

My uncle and aunt were busy most days, and my holiday was happy but full of gaps where I was by myself. Now that I was away from Dickies I felt drifting and often lonely, and I thought that this was how the Outside must be and that I would not fit into it. I went to the pictures a lot by myself, and when the days were fine I used to go down to the salt-water swimming pool and practise the crawl.

I used to wear two swimming costumes at the same time, both blue, the holes in one hiding the holes in the other. The town had a swimming gala and I put my name down for the fifty yards free style race for over-fifteens.

On the day a fine crowd was banked high alongside the pool, full of summer enthusiasm and summer colour. There were dozens of boys in the under-fifteen races, but only myself and one other youth in the overfifteen event. He was eighteen, muscled, bronzed and lithe, and I stood beside him on the edge of the bath, skinny and with my swimming costumes hanging around my middle like a droopy loin cloth.

We bent on the starting edge, the pistol cracked, we dived, and my trunks came down, all in a matter of seconds. It might seem funny now, but then it was a moment of awful horror and terrible shame, with everyone screaming with laughter as though I were the clown of the show. Somehow I pulled the trunks up around my bum and, crying tears of anger and rage at my own stupidity, I set out after my only rival who was nearly home.

He beat me by thirty yards out of fifty, and I staggered from the bath, glad that my face was wet anyway so they wouldn't see I was crying. They were still laughing, a lot of them, but I called them bleeding swines under my breath, and I went up to the rostrum to receive my prize for coming second.

The Tarzan youth had been presented with a pigskin hairbrush and comb. I got a hairbrush without a comb, which I bore proudly and happily to my uncle, and kept on the window ledge behind my bed when I returned to Dickies.

On that holiday I had tea in bed, a radio in the bedroom, lots of food and ice cream, and I nearly drowned in my cousin's canoe.

But I was alone most of the time, tied down by something that prevented me making friends. I walked by the sea and watched its gentle fingers on the pebbles. I saw the thoughtful ships come hooting up the channel, and watched the wind disturb the gulls in their curling flight.

Just to cheer myself up I went to a photographer's and had my picture taken with my coat collar turned up so that I looked like a detective.

Then, at last, I went back to Dickies and told Frank and Boz and Johnny Brice all about it, and especially about my cousin's girl with the rose in her hair.

Things had been happening at Dickies too. There had been three bunks, the film had caught fire in the projector on Saturday night, and two of the kids were in hospital after eating deadly nightshade.

'Christ, it was amazing,' said Bricey. 'In the middle of the night Wullie and Herbie suddenly get out of bed and start charging about and yelling out. They're in Little Audrey's dorm and she went to see what was happening and they tried to *do* her.'

Little Audrey was a new dormitory matron, young, bespectacled, but an improvement on most since she was shapely.

'They tried to *do* her?' I gasped. 'What happened?'

'Well,' gurgled Bricey, 'these berries they'd been scoffing are like a . . . sort of . . .'

'Love potion,' said the Professor knowledgeably. 'They had belladonna poisoning.'

'That's right,' agreed Brice. 'It made them go all mad and randy. They tried to *do* Little Audrey, straight they did.'

'Yeah,' injected Boz. 'They reckon Wullie had his

nightshirt up round his waist and was waggling his THING! It must 'ave been a scream.'

They rolled all over the beds with the laughter of telling it again, and I nearly choked and the Professor had to bang me on the back.

I was back again. This was Dickies and this was where I belonged.

13

CABBAGEPANTS DID A bunk from Dickies at least once a fortnight, pathetically but determinedly trying to get home to his mum. He was about seven or eight and he was nearly always caught the day after bunking, and returned, issuing tears and pledges never to do it again, to the stern Gaffer.

He had glowing red hair and a watery face, and he was unhappy because the other kids used to knock him about a lot and jeer at him when he cried, which was often.

There was that night when he was in the bathroom just before I did my bunk. I can still see him now sitting at one end of the bath in the inky water, and remember again the sadness and the horror of what happened afterwards.

Bathnight at Dickies, one dormitory one night, was an hour of tumult and steam; two boys to a bath, and then another pair, and another, until the water became so filthy that a bather emerged dirtier than he entered, and then it was changed. There were four fat baths, water hot enough to be just bearable, gushing steam, and boys suspended upside-down by their legs from the crossbars of the showers, which didn't work.

Competitions were held to see who could hang nakedly there for the longest time, and many a kid had slipped and dropped like a bomb on to the top of his head. Bath time was the time for comparing muscles and other parts of the anatomy, and the opportunity for events to see who could stay under water for two minutes or more. A boy called Baldy Pickins held this record until, trying to better his time against a new boy, he was dragged semi-conscious from the bath and had to surrender his title.

On the night my letter arrived I was sitting at one end of the bath, doing my neck with one of the stiff, scrubby brushes, and Cabbagepants was at the other.

His knees topped the thick water like mudflats and his face was preoccupied as ever. 'Got bashed up twice today,' he complained. 'I'm bunking from this sodding dump and they won't get me this time neither. When I get 'ome to my mum she'll not 'ave me coming back to Dickies, you watch.'

He had said it all before. In fact he was always saying it in some form or another, and I would have forgotten it just as I had the other times had it not been for my own adventure. And his.

A boy came round with the letters which must have been squatting on the Gaffer's desk since the afternoon postman. He came in, whizzing the envelopes across the room, through the steam. One flopped into the water of the next bath and the kid in there swore like mad because, as he went to grab it, he pushed it under the water and in a second it was all pulp and running ink.

I got my letter. A letter in an oval scrawl, hunchbacked across the envelope, but the stamp stuck on very carefully and straight.

First of all I half got out of the bath. Then I sat down in it again and dried my hands on somebody's towel which was on the floor. I opened it and sat in the dirty water and read what my brother Roy had written. It was a short note on a single page, which was soon filled with his big letters falling against each other as though needing support. It was strange too, for it was written in an unsurprised way, as though he had been writing regularly for the whole of the year and a half we had been parted.

I knew I would have to see him again. All the time I had thought about him and about our life when we were at home with our mother. I still had the half a tin of sweets that our brother had sent. As I got out of the bath I was working out the best day to run away and find Roy again.

He was living with foster parents in a village called Long

Crendon in Buckinghamshire. The next day I went to the public library and looked at it on the map. I thought it would be about sixty miles from Dickies and I decided that I would start out on the next Sunday.

Sometimes before this, when I had a mind to do a bunk, I would work out methods and routes and theories in my head. But I had never attempted to fulfil them. Once I planned to slip from my bed at night and hide in the loft over the stone staircase. I would stay there for a few days and nights, coming down to raid the breadroom by darkness, and then, when all the first searchings for me had finished, I would come out and deftly slip away.

At this time I even went so far as to climb through the trapdoor and into the loft in the middle of one night. Up there it was dark, with spiders and moving things. But the worst was the thin wind that wedged itself under the tiles and tried to prise them off. I shivered there for about five minutes, decided it was no place to spend days and nights and came down again.

I selected Sunday for the start of my journey to visit my brother, because it was the day we wore our suits and I thought it would be a good idea to go looking presentable. My suit was dark blue, and we had just been given a consignment of eggy yellow ties, and I had one so I thought I would wear that too. I also had my banana-coloured gloves, which I had bought in King's Lynn, and it did not occur to me that either they or the tie might make me conspicuous.

At breakfast I managed to pick up two boiled eggs instead of one, and an extra slice of bread. I had three apples and about two and eightpence.

It was the money which was troubling me. I had been without dush for a couple of weeks for some misdemeanour and two shillings and the few pence was the most I could gather. By selling some of my prized personal possessions, at bargain prices and to hard buyers who knew I wanted the money desperately, I made some funds and I managed to borrow the odd penny or twopence at school.

My original plan was to bunk immediately after breakfast, but there was a chance that the Gaffer would miss me if I didn't go to church. Today might be the day that he decided to make a check. You could never tell with the Gaffer.

So we marched to church like we did every Sunday, with the Gaffer sniffing the air along the pavement while we stepped it out in the road, and all the people stared and said 'Oooh, poor little chaps' so that you wanted to stick your tongue out at them.

Church was hollow and unholy as it always was. It was dreary, with none of the warmth of the church at Narborough, none of its comfortable, living feeling, none of its help to God. This church gave you the feeling that it was only opened on Sunday and then shut up thankfully for the rest of the week. It was a necessary evil, like Matron's Bible Class.

We used to sit in the balcony, so that we were out of the way and what was going on down below was remote. If you were far enough out of the Gaffer's eye you could read comics.

The odd thing was that the barber who used to chop off our hair would appear on the other side of the balcony, always halfway through the service, puffing and looking apologetic as though he had sinned deeply on his way there. Always the Gaffer would see him and, after privately noting the time of his arrival, would give him a quick churchy nod.

The barber was the only one who ever sat in the balcony apart from us, and sometimes I thought that perhaps he only came so that the Gaffer would see he was a church-going man and allow him to continue to cut our hair. On the other hand he may have really enjoyed his worshipping.

We returned to the regular Sunday lunch, a stone wall of jacketed potatoes piled on their tray, the expressionless cold meat and the moribund butter beans. Then the currant pudding and custard. And after that I was away.

It was my plan to cut across Richmond Park and go from there to Ealing, which was the first of the towns on the map I had drawn of my route to Long Crendon. With me I had the retired music case in which I normally carried my school books, and inside it was the hard boiled egg, the bread, the apples, a pencil and paper, and my brother's toffees in their tin. The map I had in my pocket.

It was nearly October and the day had seen the passing of

full rain clouds across the sky. As I walked over the grass of the park and under the trees, the big clouds were crowding together and it looked like rain. Lines of beech trees on the rising ground stood out like bones against the dark. Up and down the small hills and down again, so that I imagined it was the ribbed skeleton of a long and ancient animal lying there.

The grass and heather of the park were worn out from the summer and they felt old and fragile under my shoes as I went. It was not a good day and I seemed to be alone there. No people, no animals and hardly a bird. It was quiet and still and waiting for the rain.

The rain came in round, marble drops, rattling in the trees, drumming among the grass and causing the heather to tremble. The clouds seemed to be climbing on each other's backs in their hurry and the splashes joined together into a downpour. Now, I thought, was the time to go back, really. I was under a tree and none of the rain was coming on me, but now was the time to make up my mind whether to go on or not. If I returned my steps now – or anyway after the rain had stopped — there was a good chance that I would not have been missed, and I would have dodged Matron's Bible Class, which was always a good thing.

A busy stream had appeared from somewhere inside the tree, and was running down the trunk and on to the ground at my feet. But the rain eased quite quickly and I saw a man on a bicycle coming along the road from the far end of the park. He had a rigid overcoat pulled up around his head, and his neck hunched into the coat. He pedalled up the road and passed near me but he did not see me. I came from under the tree and went up to the road out of the wet grass.

Some of the sky was empty now, that distinct blue emptiness that comes after autumn or spring rain. But there were still corpulent black clouds, and one especially big with the sun shining at the back of it and the beams flung out as though God himself were behind it. I reached the road and turned towards Richmond because I had decided to go on.

The journey to my brother lasted about five days. I walked a good part of the way, resting away from the road every so often in a field or a lane. Twice I got good long lifts, once on a lorry and once in a van, but the driver of the van misunderstood the place I wanted to go and I went miles astray.

He did not ask me where I had come from, nor did he seem to need to know anything else about me. He was a young man in blue overalls, and he whistled through his teeth all the time we were travelling.

Then when the lorry stopped the driver had a big bundle of a dog in the cab. 'If you want a lift you'll have to get on the back,' he said. Then he laughed and called after me: 'That's if you can stand it.'

I climbed on to the back of the lorry and I understood what he meant. He had been around the countryside collecting swill for pigs. There were six or seven bins full of it and it slopped and flopped over the side as the road bent and the lorry jumped. The smell unfurled behind the bins, fluttering like a banner, and although I crouched right on the tailboard, with my head hanging over the side, I could still not avoid it.

At nights, during the journey, I slept twice under bridges; once under a railway bridge and once under a bridge across a river with a small path where the arch and water touched. There was a leaf-shaped boat pulled up on the path and a tarpaulin in the boat. I lay in the boat, and it rained outside the bridge and the rain slipped off the arch and into the river making a noise like a waterfall. Even when the rain stopped I couldn't sleep because it dripped into the river all night.

On the other two nights I slept in country bus shelters, on the benches, with my collar pulled right up and my face turned away from the road so that it would not show up white to anyone passing.

It was strange, for no one bothered me all the time I was on my way. You might have thought that a boy in a deformed blue suit, with a yellow tie, yellow gloves and a music case, might have attracted some curiosity, but I did not. I made sure that I did not look too vagabond by carefully washing in a stream or river as soon as I could each day, combing my hair and trying to keep my shirt and tie straight.

Before I had set out the thought that worried me most was that I might get so hungry that I would have to give myself up.

But on the road I had no anxiety because there were orchards still bushelled with fruit, and it lay clustered in the autumn grass under the hedgerows. There were still blackberries in the thorns, and I collected ears of wheat, left lying in open fields after the harvesting, and munched it as I went.

In Wendover I bought a loaf of bread from a woman in a baker's shop who looked at me in a strange way, and I bought a couple of buns the next day from another place.

It was a fine journey really. It did not rain very much in the day and although I got tired I was never sad. I found that if you did not think of the steps you were pacing, or count the miles too diligently, the places you aimed for seemed to arrive so quickly that they might have set out themselves to meet you half-way.

There was plenty to see and think about. There were grey and red houses sitting like resting travellers at the roadside and others by themselves up on the brows of the gentle Chilterns. I wondered why people should build houses like that, away and alone, with a valley and perhaps a wood between them and their neighbours. I would see a house like that, and imagine the man going gladly home in the evening and sitting out in front for a while and watching anything that was going on below. Or perhaps just sitting and watching nothing in particular but the light going off fields and the late sky and the dull shining of a river or stream.

Two of the afternoons turned warm and I got dusty and dry as I walked. My toes were uncomfortable too because my shoes were a bit small and my toes were always a funny collection anyway, all pushed and bunched together like people in a bus.

Autumn showed most in the trees. Where they stood together in woods or copses they were like girls standing together, each girl with a different colour hair.

Some of the fields were already turned and tilled, brown and vacant, with birds sitting on the furrows.

Sometimes, as I went, I would think about words. Not in any context or sentence, not in any poem or rhyme. But words for themselves alone, for what they were, simple and coloured and fine, each one a poem or a picture.

Fall for autumn, sorrel for a horse, burnished for what the trees were. Just words. Lonely, loftily, topsail, reef, mist, oleander, isthmus, seascape, widgeon, conifer, quadrille, wild and wanderlust. Largo in music, sonnet in reading, Curaçao, Cayenne and Lourenço Marques for places that were far away.

Once, at the roadside, there was a timbered cottage alongside a stone wall, like an old ship lying at a jetty.

The roof had sighed and sagged in the middle and moss and ivy lived on the walls and windowsills. It looked, I thought then, the sort of house that had wanted lots of things doing to it for years; a comfortable house, a place where the man never quite got around to getting things done. The garden was a nice, random affair too, as though he had put the flowers and the plants in the piece of ground that happened to be nearest his hand at the time. He had not even bothered to take the deck chair in from the grass. It had been out all the summer, you could tell that by its faded face. Now the rain had soaked it and it nursed dying leaves in its lap.

At home, at home with my mother I mean, we had always *tried* to have a garden. I had worked hard in it but somehow it had never grown. In the front garden there was the infirm climber clinging desperately to the brick wall, and this my mother always referred to as 'the dog rose tree.' We also had some irises which appeared like a miracle every year, some jungled grass and a privet hedge. In the middle of the grass I had once cut and dug a rectangular flower bed, but the pink, fluffy woman who used to come to tea and tell my mother's fortune saw it and leaned over to me and said: 'It shouldn't be there, boy. It looks just like a grave.'

Terrified, I replaced all the turves of grass I had removed and then it looked more like a grave than ever. So I pulled them up again and frantically dug the whole garden over. After that it rained and the place became a morass.

At the back the garden was a bit longer, starting at the kitchen door and terminating at the boards that fenced us off from the engine sheds. Every spring I dug the thick ground and planted potatoes and lettuces and dwarf beans, and some of them grew.

The man next door gave me some strawberry plants and they produced three strawberries in the summer of 1942. My brother ate all three at one go and I got him on the ground and punched him until my mother came out and pulled us apart.

When we heard that the Government were going to provide us with air-raid shelters I dug a substantial hole at the bottom of the garden to receive ours, imagining at every exhausting spadeful that this was my war effort. Then some men came along, dug another hole at the top of the garden and placed the air-raid shelter in it. My hole remained there forever, a wadi in summer, a pool in the rains, and a place for drifting snow in the deep of winter.

As I walked towards Long Crendon, through the strange countryside and the unknown towns, I wondered how Roy would look now. It was a year and a half since I had stumbled from the ambulance with the woman promising that I would see him again the next day, and left him sitting up puzzled on the stretcher, with his small bundle of belongings on the floor.

It was in the late afternoon that I saw my first signpost with 'Long Crendon' on it. I was tired and there was a wind walking about in the trees; an autumn wind throwing birds and clouds about in the sky and singing a song of a cold night to come.

Long Crendon, said the signpost, was ten miles. Walking, weary as I now was, I knew I would never get there that night. It meant sleeping once more in some rough place, cold and aching and afraid again, listening for footsteps and watching for headlights on the road.

I walked for about half a mile up the road which went from the signpost.

Then I stopped, and stood in the hedge for a while and watched a police car parked two hundred yards further on. Presently a policeman appeared, turned the car around and drove off in the other direction. I went cautiously along through the briars and the ditches and came opposite the place where the car had been. It was a country police station, a house really, with a yard, a notice board, and a garage.

For a moment I had a suspicious, and thrilling, feeling that my picture might be on the notice board with the word 'Wanted' above it, and a full description, down to my yellow tie and my banana gloves, beneath. But there was no notice and nobody seemed to be about either, just the wind sweeping the yard and brushing the hedges and boughs.

At the moment when I was about to walk on, giving myself a mental warning to keep a watch for the police car returning, I noticed a shed at the side of the yard. Its roof slid low and it was open at the front. Inside were half a dozen bicycles.

It was a few strides across the yard. I took the bike that came first, which was also the oldest and most cranky, this being some saver for my conscience.

I ran with it across the yard and out into the road where I mounted it. It worked. It went. Apart from a tendency for the saddle to slip from side to side with each movement of the legs, it worked and went fine.

Joyously now I rode, my music case hanging from the handle-bars, the old bike going along like a charger suddenly freed from a stable. I knew the wind was with me for I could feel it pushing behind my ears, and pummelling my back, and the grey clouds raced along above me like a hunting pack.

Once the music case slipped and fell on to the road, the tin of toffees inside it clanging as it hit the ground. The bike had no working brakes, I discovered at that moment, and I had to scrape along with my feet before I could stop it. Then, a few minutes later, a car rounded a curve far ahead and, thinking it was the homing police car, I swerved the bike recklessly from the road, collided with a gate and completed the spectacular movement by somersaulting from the saddle into the field.

The car went past without stopping and I was crouching in the hedge at that time, so I did not know whether it was the police car or not.

I pushed off again, the way the clouds were running. The figures on the signposts diminished. At last there was one which said 'Long Crendon 1 mile.'

It was evening everywhere now, broken clouds over broken fields, with the trees becoming smudgy and merged, early lights in far windows and smoke curling like locks of dark hair. The road led straight into the village. I had never been there before and I never went there again, but I remember a big field with a low wall skirting it, and the road running along by the wall.

My brother was walking across the field, diagonally towards the road, as I pedalled along by the wall. Even though there was dusk and a year and a half between us, I knew it was Roy.

'Roy! Roy! Roy! Roy!' I don't know how many times I called, or why I kept calling like that, because he heard me first time and he knew it was me because he cried back and raced towards the gate in the wall.

He was running and I was pedalling, and I got there first, but the bike was going at such a pace that it slid beneath me and careered on as I jumped off. I fell over, then got up again, just as he was running to the gate.

He was not much different really, a bit taller, but skinny still, and grinning with his broken tooth at the front, and his hair straight down over his eyes. He climbed on the gate and dropped over.

We just stood, facing each other, neither of us knowing what to do next. My instinct was to put my arms around him because he was my brother and I loved him dearly, but boys don't do that sort of thing easily. And it seemed too formal, too grown up, to shake hands. That would have been just as foolish.

So I said: ''lo Roy.'

''ello Les,' he said.

'Here,' I said, fumbling in my music case. 'I've got some toffees for you.'

Because they had not liked his name, his foster parents called him George. This made me angry at the time, and still does. It was not sufficient that he, at nine years of age, should suddenly be taken from everything he knew, but after going through the pipeline of the system he should find himself with a new name.

His foster parents were kind country people with a small house where they made me a bed on the landing. But to them he was George, and at school he was George. It reeked of injustice to me. Roy, after all, was good enough for his first mother.

I sat on the end of his bed for hours that night and we talked quietly like two mice. Talked of all the days we had known together, and the days since, and all that had happened. He had been the most unhappy after we had been parted, and he kept writing letters to our mother and getting no reply. When the Martin family went to see him and told him that she had been dead for a year he had cried, but felt relieved in an odd way too, because he had thought that she did not want to have anything to do with him any more.

He was content now in this small place. It was strange to hear him call the woman in the house Mum, and to hear him say that his father was a thatcher. He talked of villages around the countryside, and boys at school, and summer cricket matches, and how they had been down to Marlow and the Thames for a holiday. All the things we had known, the lamp-post games on winter nights, the dusty street in August, the Ebbw coal we cut from the black river bank, our friends and foes, our parents and the big black and white cat, were all of a different time and a different place, and would never be ours again.

But he was no stranger to me, nor I to him. For this I was happy and thankful. I had often wondered if he would still be my brother when I found him again. And he was.

On the following day I took the bike from the front door and returned the way I had come. Roy's foster parents did not ask me how I had made the journey, and I did not tell them, nor him.

Roy walked down to the wall and the gate with me. We knew that we would never lose each other again. He climbed on the wall and waved as I went away, and he was still waving as I turned the bend in the road and left the village behind.

Easily now I pedalled back to the police station, swerved into the yard spectacularly, and replaced the cycle in the little shed with the others. I am certain that no one ever knew it was missing, certainly no one mentioned it to me.

I went to the door of the police station and gave myself up. A surprised-looking policeman with no helmet, and a cup of coffee in his hand, saw me standing there.

'I'm wanted by the police,' I said dramatically.

'Oh are you,' he said, taking a drink of coffee. 'Well it looks like we've found you don't it.'

Actually he'd never heard of me, which was a bit disappointing, but I had a fine lunch there, and a good tea in the afternoon, before they took me back to Dickies in a police car.

I was apprehensive as the journey was getting towards its end. After all I had been away nearly a week and the Gaffer had been known to be tough about things like that. But at the door of Dickies one of the staff matrons accepted me, and sent me upstairs for a bath. She said hardly anything at all and after I had bathed I was told to go to bed.

When the kids came up to the dormitory old Boz sat on the side of the bed and said: 'Did you 'ear about Cabbagepants?'

'Did he bunk?' I said, slightly hurt that he hadn't asked me about my adventure.

'That's right,' he whispered. 'He did a bunk all right. Got on the railway line somehow last night, and a train came along and killed him. Joe Errington's just been up to see the body.'

14

ALL THE DAYS spun on, full of the things of our life, so full that their passing went unnoticed until they had queued and crowded into weeks and months and then into years. Red summer days, and spring rain on the windows. White winter moons and the coldness of November. Christmases and outings, harvest festivals and the thankful marrows, books and music and fights, and Saturday night picture shows in the gym with the Gaffer looking on ready to stop the film the moment it became too sexy.

And all the time, as you grew from being just a boy, you made plans for the time when you went through the gate for the last time and the Outside was waiting. Sometimes they were more fears than plans. Fears that life, on your own, would be too difficult, that people out there would stare.

There was a small builder, I remember, who came to do some work at Dickies, and saw us and what we were, and were like, for a few weeks. Then he said: 'You're a lot of little bastards. If a kid from this place came to me for a job I'd close the cash box quick and throw him out in the road.'

When you thought about it, perhaps when you were in bed and imagining what might happen in the end, you wondered how many people there were who would throw you into the road.

Social contacts with outsiders were not encouraged unless

they had offered, and after being vetted, had been allowed to take you on some outing on a Saturday or Sunday. Of course you were on your best behaviour and they were frequently quite as nervous and unsure as you, like someone taking a new dog for a walk, so neither they nor you learned much.

But sometimes something came from one of these insubstantial people which was a blessing for every one of us. A kid called Seek, who slept on the far row of the dormitory, one Saturday returned with a mouth full of chocolate and an old book which some benefactor had given him.

He was a boy of moods and occasional ages of silence. On this evening he stayed a long time with the book, crouching and shifting on his bed. The person who had taken him out had also given him five shillings and on the following Monday Seek appeared with a boxful of electrical bits. He emptied them on the floor of the gym, in a corner, and proceeded to assemble, from a diagram in the book, a crystal radio set. Coil and condenser, crystal and catswhisker were put together. Then he bought a pair of earphones, promising to pay the indulgent shopkeeper weekly.

We had laughed at him while he was putting it together, but on the day he brought the earphones home we all stood around the bed while he fixed the wires on the terminals. His face was set and anxious, for he had striven hard for this and all his hopes were in it.

Some of the kids were scoffing at him still, but most of us kept quiet and watched. He had scratched some of the black paint off his iron bedrail, and looped the aerial wire around it, so that the whole bed, ingeniously, became an aerial. The earth wire was hooked around some pipes at the back of the bed.

When he had fixed the earphones, he clamped them around his doubting face like a halo, winced his eyes up tight, and listened. Nothing. His expression told us that. Then he reached forward and moved the catswhisker wire across the small, silver rock of the crystal. Its point scratched gently, like the feeler of an insect.

He had bent low like a worshipper. Then swiftly he straightened, joy and wonder and astonishment all moving in his face and in his eyes.

'It's going! I can 'ear it!' he exclaimed with a triumphant exultation that Marconi might have remembered. 'Listen! It's music. Taa tum tum taa tum . . .'

We were all bouncing around the bed now like puppets on excited strings. 'Come on, then, let's 'ear it,' someone shouted. Seek struggled out of the earphones and as soon as he did the sound of music was so loud that we could all hear it at once. The earphones were lying on the bed, in the middle of the grey blanket, and the tune was coming from them. Taa tum tum taa tum. . . .

That was just the beginning. Within a week there were coggie sets, as they became called, all over the home. Boys lay half suffocating under their blankets until midnight, in secret delight listening to dance music, to Tommy Handley, to the news. A sudden new world seemed to spring up and expand for us. We whistled and sang the latest songs, and talked about the plays we had heard. Seek, the aptly named, had found something of great value.

Nobody in authority knew that the listening went on until the BBC's final goodnight. Dormitory matrons did their usual nightly prowls without detecting anything more than regularly sleeping boys, unaware that beneath the blankets the laughter evoked by some radio comedian was only being smothered with immense difficulty.

I shared a coggie set with Frank Knights who slept on one side of me. It was a good one and we had two pairs of earphones – or eardogs as they were named – fixed to it. Every morning, if you had the eardogs under your pillow you could hear Big Ben at six o'clock.

Sometimes I could lie and listen to music while I looked up through the glazed bit in the window and watched all the fullness of the night sky. With music as my wings I felt sometimes that I could soar there with the cloudy stars and the melodious moon. The Planets Suite I loved because I could imagine each one a god riding by on prancing horses. And Fingal's Cave, all loneliness and longing. And Morning, a Bare Mountain, Peter and the Wolf and a Calm Sea and a Prosperous Voyage.

I travelled with them all, taken by the music that came

through the earphones to enchanted places. In the morning I was always dead beat.

But even the precious coggie set was not so prized that it could not be sacrificed when the occasion came about. And it did. It was because of a girl.

Boz and I, and some of the others, were invited to a social evening in Surbiton and we arrived there stiff as sandwichmen in our best suits and plastered hair. We stood about, scratching ourselves secretly and feeling we had come to the wrong place. Some motherly ladies, heavy with bosoms and scent, gave us sandwiches, sausage rolls and cakes. Then a funny man got on the floor and picked out one of our boys and asked him to go out and join him.

'What's your name?' the funny man asked.

'Willie Dye,' said the boy truthfully.

'Will He Die!' exploded the funny man. 'Of course he will!'

He collapsed with the weight of his own wit. Nearly everyone thought the joke was hilarious, and they bent themselves all over the place with the laughing. Except us. Because it was a pun we'd finished with in Dickies years ago.

'Will he die!' chortled the funny man again.

'Will'e arse 'oles,' shouted Boz, who became annoyed very easily, and was now.

Shocked, staggered, outraged, delighted, overwhelmed. The reactions flapped around the room from face to face. Boz stood his ground and glared at the funny man. Then a lady who was standing near the food gave Boz two doughnuts to pacify him, someone started some music and we were driven into the middle of the floor to join the outer of two circles, revolving there around each other.

'When the music stops you dance with the person who is opposite you,' cooed the lady who had given Boz the buns.

My stomach turned to milk because I'd never danced a step in my life. But it was already too late. The music stopped and I was standing opposite her. She was about fourteen, rounded and pretty, with a river of gentle hair falling over her neck and shoulders. I was unable to move, but the music was jolting again and she stepped forward and said: 'We have got to dance.'

153

'But I can't,' I said miserably, putting my arms out to her nevertheless.

'Nor me, very much,' she said. 'Never mind, we'll sort of walk. What was that your friend shouted out?'

'Nothing. Not really,' I said. 'He has funny shouting fits, like an epileptic, you know. And he has to shout something. But it don't mean anything.'

'He's all right now,' she said, glancing towards the edge of activity where Boz was chewing the doughnuts and grinning wickedly because he was not involved in the dancing.

'Yes,' I agreed piously. 'He's soon over them, thank God. What are we s'posed to be dancing?'

She wasn't sure, but she said her name was Helen and she had a friend called Kathleen and they often went to the pictures in Kingston. I took a plunge from a great and frightening height and said I'd like to take her to the pictures, and I could bring along a friend who could take her friend. She said she would.

When we got back to Dickies that night, I woke up Frank Knights. He half sat up, stared at me through the dark, and I said: ''Ere, guess what? I've got a date.'

He sprang up, immediately wide eyed. 'With a woman?' he said.

''Course,' I said proudly. 'Met her tonight. You ought to see her. She's cracking, Frank, honest she is.'

'You didn't kiss 'er or anything like that?'

'Not yet. But I'm taking her to the pictures. *And* I've fixed you up with her friend.'

'YOU HAVEN'T,' he cried out with great joy. 'You've got one for me too! What's mine like?'

'Shut up,' I said. 'You'll wake old Chuck up.'

'Well then,' he whispered fiercely, 'what's mine like? I've got a right to know. After all she's my woman.'

'I don't know what she's like,' I admitted. 'Only mine was there tonight. But yours is called Kathleen and she's fourteen like Helen, who is my one.'

'When's the date?' he asked.

'Saturday,' I whispered. 'Six o'clock at the bus garage.'

'That's smashing,' he gurgled in the dark. 'You're a good mate.' He was quiet for a bit. Then he said: 'All we need now is some money.'

'How are we going to get that?' I asked.

He didn't answer right away, but stretched out his tall, bony body on the mattress and stared up as though trying to see the ceiling through the dark.

'There's only one thing to do,' he said deliberately, having thought long about it. 'We'll have to flog the coggie set.'

I was considerably shocked at this. I thought of the late, quiet hours, and the music, and the announcer telling you what had happened in Berlin or Baghdad, and what the

weather was going to be like. It was a lot to sacrifice. Then I imagined her again, with the small nose and the nice eyes, and the falling hair. And I thought about us in the dark of the pictures, me with my arm about her, perhaps touching her hair with my fingers.

'Right,' I said. ' 'We'll flog it.'

The next morning Frank sat on the edge of his bed, dressing very slowly. 'I had a dream about mine last night,' he said. 'I can hardly wait for Saturday. I reckon we'll get ten bob for the coggie set.'

As it happened we made even a better bargain. Porky Blake had just got another postal order from his auntie and the Gaffer had not spotted it. And he wanted a coggie set.

'We wouldn't do this for any guy in the place,' Frank told him. 'But we've got these couple of hot women, see, and we're going out with them. So we need the dush.'

We got twelve and six out of him, and with our own pocket money the total fund available for our date was seventeen and six.

On the Friday we both had hair cuts and on Saturday at ten to six we waited on the corner just a little distance from the bus garage.

'We won't wait right on the spot,' said Frank in a voice heavy with experience. 'Let them get there first. We don't want them to see us hanging around waiting. It's better to treat women rough.'

At six o'clock we decided to wait at the bus garage after all. The buses nosed in and out, the people went past, there was a man playing a shining trumpet in the gutter. Two girls walked nearly up to us at quarter past and Frank went stumbling towards them, and I had to pull him back and tell him it wasn't them.

By seven o'clock we knew they weren't coming. Our dream of fair women died with the strokes of the clock. We kicked around for a while and then we began to walk slowly back towards Dickies.

'I fancied that Kathleen too,' sighed Frank unhappily.

'How?' I said. 'You never even saw 'er.'

'Well I just fancied her that's all. I got really fond of her after that dream. What's it matter anyway.'

Just then we slouched by a pea-green café with the menu pinned up and flapping on the door like a white hand. Frank stopped and examined it.

'You hungry?' he asked.

I stared at him. I had never in all my life had a meal in a restaurant.

' 'Course I am,' I said. 'But . . .'

'Let's have a scoff,' he said, and opened the door and marched in.

It was empty except for a waitress sitting in one corner, her nose an inch from the evening paper. Every table had a nice paper tablecloth on it, with a little island fortress of salt, pepper and bottles of sauce, Heinz tomato and HP, in the middle.

We had sausages, eggs, and double chips, a piled plate of bread and margarine, and two cups of leather-coloured tea each. When we had finished we were full. I looked across to him and grinned. 'There's always plenty of women about,' I said philosophically.

'Bags of them,' he grinned wickedly. 'Good scoff wasn't it?'

'Cracking,' I said. We got the bill for five and twopence, paid it splendidly and left a whole sixpence for the waitress. Then we walked up Kingston Hill and home.

It was dark so we knew we could get over the fence without being seen, and we would have to because we were late out.

Frank jerked himself up the fence and dropped easily over the other dark side. We crouched there together waiting in case anyone was about. We could see the lights in the dormitories across the vacant black of the mudpatch.

'I'll tell you what,' said Frank.

'What?' I said.

'I'll bet she was terrible. Bosky and with big goggles, and legs thick all the way down.'

He laughed and I laughed with him. Then we ran swiftly, but with stealth, across the mudpatch towards the dormitory.

People were always sending things to Dickies. Some of the gifts were sound and useful, but a lot of them were not, the donors apparently regarding us as merely an extension to the rubbish dump. The Gaffer would sigh his profound, croaking sigh as yet another diseased bicycle was brightly handed in at the door by someone who thought the poor little boys might like to play with it. Sometimes they even wanted a receipt or a letter of thanks.

Christmas each year brought always a plague of trash, chewed up books, bats without handles, a torment of jigsaw puzzles with missing bits, and long exploded chemistry sets.

One serene giver appeared at the front door dressed as Father Christmas, and clanging a bell, to hand in a whole mountain of worthless wreckage that was burning in the boiler even before he had proceeded on his merry way down Kingston Hill.

Another Christmas Eve saw the Gaffer crouched in his office, picking away at his typewriter, accompanied by a stuffed and nasty-looking weasel, half a ton of custard powder, and a Princess Margaret Doll's House, the sort of things that are always useful in a home for a hundred and fifty boys.

Each dormitory matron had the task of picking out one gift for each of her boys from a pile of toys deposited in the chapel on Christmas Eve. There were many good gifts as well as the rubbish, and most boys got something of value.

One Christmas morning I found a view-finder thing on the bottom of my bed. You fitted in pictures (in this case slightly yellowed views of the Lake District) into a frame and looked at them through the eye-pieces, whereupon they fused into a lifelike scene.

Within an hour I had travelled through Ullswater, Windermere and Grasmere, gazed through the window of Wordsworth's cottage, and become thoroughly bored with the whole process. Fortunately a boy in another dormitory recognised my Christmas gift as his property which had been stolen from him some time previously, and had presumably found its way into the Gaffer's office, and been dished out again with the other stuff.

I argued that it was legitimately mine, but agreed to sell it back to him for one and six, which I did, so everyone was satisfied.

Not at Christmas, but some other time of the year, someone brought to Dickies a gramophone, which worked, and some records. Frank had just been given a room of his own because he was sixteen, and it was to his room, at the dark top of the Death Row corridor, that he bore the gramophone.

For weeks there floated down the stone corridor, echoing to the kitchen, the wailing of a song called Isle of Dreams and a crippled version of Offenbach's *La Belle Hélène*. Two other records were broken at an early stage, but the other two Frank preserved jealously. They were played twenty times a day, until the grooves had grown deep and the needle dimmed, and the gramophone itself, elderly though willing as it was, groaned to a stop one evening and died of overwork.

It was in this cell of a room with its pale, cold, brick walls, and the wire guard over the window to prevent cricket balls from the playground breaking through, that Frank and I produced Dickies' own newspaper. It sold at a penny a copy and ran twice a week for a couple of months until we went broke.

It started life as a wall-newspaper, hanging in two big sheets in the chapel, retelling the week's news of the home and at school, with cartoons by Frank, and a short story by me. There was also a rhyme by an erudite boy called Medhurst, who was very good at poems, most often completely unprintable. We had the programme for the Saturday night cinema show and divulged who had been selected for the next football game.

Such was the success of this that we decided to print individual copies and sell them. There was a jelly substance which could be bought by the tin, boiled in the kitchen and spread over a tin tray. Then you wrote your page of the newspaper in special ink, and, when the jelly was set, you laid it on the tray. The ink sank into the jelly and from then on you printed copies of the page by laying them across the inked surface for a few minutes each. Our circulation limit was forty because by that time the jelly was frayed, the ink exhausted, and the print sprawled and splodged over the page.

'Sell the good copies to the big kids,' said Frank, who was a good businessman, 'and the rotten copies to the little 'uns because they won't ask for their money back if they can't read it.'

The paper sold well. We began to serialise, without permission because we didn't know we needed it, *The Monkey's Paw*. One day we got to a sentence which said that one character had chased another around the room with an antimacassar.

'What's an antimacassar?' I asked Frank as I copied from the book on to our printing paper.

'Never heard of it,' he said. 'None of the kids here will know. Change it to teapot.'

So I did.

We initiated an essay competition with a sixpenny prize for the best effort each week. The first week we got an entry headed: 'Why The Gaffer Is A Bastard,' written anonymously by someone who elaborated on the theme with considerable observation.

Frank was all for printing it, but I said the Gaffer would close us down. So we scrapped it and awarded the prize to a kid called Ginger Edmunds who, with a sweet ignorance of both biology and history, had written an epic entitled: 'My Dad Was Killed in the First War.' We gave him the sixpence and his eyes shone behind his glasses as he took it.

The literary side of the paper was blooming and we were selling it to people outside as well as inside the home. But the technical problems of production were burdening us. Boil it as we might the jelly, once it became overworked, it smelled like seaweed and refused to jell. It was expensive, about four shillings a tin, so that on the jelly alone we were eightpence in the red with every issue.

We could not increase the price of our paper because we did not think the Dickie guys would buy it for twopence. Not unless it was a better production.

With this in mind I went to a jobbing printer in Kingston. I told him that I was thinking of giving him the contract for printing our home magazine and asked him to name his price. He had a green apron and a greenish face too, with stubble on his chin. I couldn't make up my mind whether he was laughing at me behind his green face or not. He said he would have to go into more detail, but he thought it would cost about fifty pounds a month to make a decent job of the magazine.

I felt my knees give a twitch and I looked at him hard. But he had a straight face. So I said: 'I'll have to put it to the editor. We'll let you know if we accept your estimate.' Then I picked up my school satchel and staggered out, sad because I knew our newspaper was dead.

15

WHEN THE GAFFER finally went his way it was like the sinking of an old, lean, wooden ship. He had been eager for his retirement for years, but as it approached he grew silent and fidgety and no longer spoke of the hollyhocks he was going to nurture along his Cornish garden fence.

But his age was telling. Boys he pursued, when he chanced on them breaking the law, could now outdistance him, leaving him holding his ribs and giving small puffs into his thin cheeks like touches of wind in the sails of the old wooden ship. He still threatened a good bit, but he did not seem to have the energy or the will to carry out his threats.

If any proof were needed that he was growing soft it came one morning when Spikey Thorn, who was one of the regular skivvies over at Matron's cottage, approached the Gaffer in the dining hall with penitent tears hanging like icicles from his eye lashes.

'I've been and gone and killed the budgie, sir,' said Spikey, dissolving into plunging sobs at the awful words he uttered.

'It's stone dead, sir, in the bottom of the cage.'

The Gaffer sat paralysed. The budgie was Matron's verbal foil, her friend and her confessor, to whom she read bits from the letters she wrote to her dear old boys. Matron was away for a few days and her companion was lying slain.

'Are you sure he's dead?' said the Gaffer in a pale voice. 'He's not just sleeping?'

'No sir,' trembled Thorn. 'I shot 'im dead with my cata-pult.'

We had all known times when Spikey would have been smitten with a single blow, and we all sat stiff with interest to see if the Gaffer would deliver it. But he did nothing but utter an uncharacteristic 'Blimey' and leaned back on his hard chair.

Thorn, it appeared, had been shooting dried peas around Matron's sitting room with his catapult, and Joey, the budgie, had made an ill-timed jump on to his perch at the very moment when one of these small, stony missiles was approaching. It had executed him quickly and efficiently and he had dropped to the floor of the cage.

'We'll have to get another bird,' said the Gaffer decisively. 'We'll get another one just the same so that she won't notice the difference. Matron is a bit short-sighted and one budgie looks like another.' He looked at Spikey with something of the old glint in his eye and said: 'And you're going to pay for it, son.'

They bought another bird, but trying to pass it off as Joey, even to Matron all screwed up behind rimless spectacles, was like trying to disguise a navvy as a prima donna. The new pet was a labourer-type budgie, whereas Joey had chirped, and while Matron's late pet had been master of an extensive and pure vocabulary, the new bird could say only one word and that was indecent.

The Gaffer, I like to remember, never revealed the full dramatic story of Joey's going, so Spikey was not condemned as a murderer in Bible Class and was not dismissed to ever-lasting hellfire.

Just after this Matron suffered a stroke and when she was sufficiently well to be moved the Gaffer, as gentlemanly and loving to her as he had been his whole life through, took her away to the cottage by the sea in Cornwall.

There she died, and in no great time he followed her.

Things began to change for us, our lives widened and we saw, as we grew older, the way we were going. The terrible doubt that we would not be able to accept the outside world, quite apart from it accepting us, the thought that I should never be able to write for a living, the other uncertainties, were settled for us.

Frank was sent to a school of art because he wanted to be a commercial artist. I left school and Barnardo's with astonishing promptitude arranged for me to take a journalism course in a college on the other side of London.

One of the elderly guard did say to me with a sort of dissuasive contempt: 'Whatever do you want to have anything to do with newspapers for? Why don't you have a nice job in insurance or something?'

But the light shone in the right places and it was fixed for me to go to the college. I would have to wait for a term, but I would go there.

In the empty four months of waiting I worked in the office at Dickies, practising my shorthand and typing, learned at nightschool, counting bread coupons which were always thousands short of the amount of bread delivered at the order of Mr Paul, the new superintendent.

That last summer too some of us went to the Isle of Man for an idyllic holiday in a gentle white house beside the road at Lazayre. It was a house looking through veils of glistening ivy, cushioned all about by patterned flowers, and sheltered by spread trees.

Years later I stopped outside that house late on an August night, and walked to the gate, thrilled by the memory it brought. Its white walls glowed through the ivy and the summer garden was moving with sweet, warm, heavy smells, and nocturnal creatures.

There hung an iron gate, its bars like strong but friendly fingers, and I knew that if I opened it and walked down between the scented stock and under the shadowy boughs, I would come to a rough cobbled yard and a line of frowning stables. Then across an angled field and to the green banks of our summer river there, a slim river, the Sulby, clear and quick and running over stones, always saying strange things and making funny faces.

On those days when we were there we would go with the girls to the river and splash in its shallows. The girls came from another home, they were our ages, and we spent that month finding out about them and them about us.

We who had lived in the jagged male world of the Kingston

home viewed them with consuming interest; wondrous creatures who ran and walked and swam with us, and who had pale skins and deep eyes and whose bodies dipped and gently swelled in disturbing fashion. In thirty days we went through the heartaches and singing joys of our first real love affairs, and for some of us our first, second and third.

There was a good, strong hill, sitting across the road from our house, the last high ground before the island flattened out to its northern plain that runs up to the Point of Ayre. The hill had a coat of smooth grass, so silken that you could take a tin tray and toboggan from crest to foot in one abandoned run.

In a smoky house near the bottom of the hill lived Mr Quale, the farmer, who had a face like fire and who had never been to England. He used to cuss us deliciously when we got in the way of his horses in the harvest field, and one night he came over and drank cocoa in our glowing kitchen and told us tales of the Manx ghosts and hobgoblins and pixies.

We returned from that summer and soon the wind began to chill and it was autumn again. In the office at Dickies, I practised my typing and counted the bread coupons, and, more often, crowded myself to the fire with a book.

On Monday mornings in November, with spidery rain and webbed mist outside, the rest of the boys would slope off to school and I would be inside with the fire cheerful and the light on, enjoying the island feeling of warmth and safeness. The brief day was gone again by the time they came home and I went with them to tea. We had toast now, and fruit, and cake, and tea with sugar in it, and cups and saucers instead of mugs.

Some evenings in the week I used to go to night-school and sit among the girls doing shorthand and thumping rhythmically at typewriters while a gramophone wheezed 'Colonel Bogey.' After the first embarrassment I did not mind being with girls, in fact I knew they were interesting. There was one girl, about sixteen, who used to talk with me about music. I asked her in a casual way if she would like to come to the Albert Hall with me. With a rapid horror I heard her say that she would love to come, and if I gave her my home number she would telephone me next day and confirm it.

I mumbled out Dickies' telephone number and went home through the night with a weighted mind wondering how I was going to speak to her undetected from the office, and, more difficult, how I was going to raise the cash to take her to the Albert Hall.

The first problem was no more easily solved than the second. I sat next to the telephone all the next morning, as close and attentive as if it were a wealthy granny on her deathbed. Each time it rang I gave a guilty leap and answered it with the number instead of saying 'Doctor Barnardo's,' which was the usual way, because I did not want her to know I came from Dickies.

There were an agonising lot of calls that morning, but eventually she rang and I stuttered into the phone, screwing my eyes around to see if Miss Blott, the new Matron, was looking. If she noted my conversation she never mentioned it, but that would be like her. Things had changed all round.

The girl came from Surbiton and she had a little, pointed Surbiton voice, that, had I known it then, spoke of innumerable sets on the tennis courts then unplayed, and gin and oranges by the gallon in future years, not to mention triumphs in amateur drama and thrilling hours of bridge.

But, to me then, she sounded complete sophistication and cool poise. A woman, not just a girl, and I was making a real, adult date.

'I don't want the cook to hear this,' I whispered into the phone, still squinting desperately at Matron. 'She carries tales all over the house. But I'll meet you at seven outside the Albert Hall.'

She did not sound very awed that I lived in a house with a cook, which was disappointing, but at least, I told myself, it was true.

Next I pondered the financial problem. I was getting five shillings a week pocket money then, but I calculated I would need at least fifteen shillings to cover the cost of this adventure. So I went to Mr Paul, the new superintendent, who was a young man and understood a lot of things, and told him I was keen to go to a concert at the Albert Hall and I wondered if I could have three weeks' pocket money in advance.

After a very little thought he agreed, and I took my cash and went joyfully to the concert. Actually he continued paying my pocket money every week and when eventually I suggested that I should repay the loan he told me to forget it.

My girl was waiting, a trifle impatiently because she was like that. But she looked nice with her dark hair and her red coat and her high-heeled shoes. As I went to buy the tickets I felt as big and confident as though I came from Surbiton too. She made a small pouting face when I bought two tickets for the remotest gods, and she grumbled all the way up the stairs, pointing out that at this rate we would never have time for a drink before the concert began.

Everything inside me froze when I heard her say this. Frantically I began counting the coins in my pocket so that I could buy her drinks. Fool! Why hadn't I realised that? Of course she would want drinks. You couldn't just take a woman to a concert and expect her to be satisfied with that. You had to think of other things and other expenses. Like drinks.

Every step up to the gallery was a stony misery. I delayed her for a while by pretending to have to do up my shoelaces,

and to my wild relief this took up an essential minute, for when we got to our seats by the rail and the awful chasm, the orchestra was just beginning to tune.

We were a long way up, so far that you could count the bald heads in the audience and the orchestra with ease. We peered over the cliff as the conductor arrived, and was immediately partially obscured by a small skein of smoke which wriggled across just below us.

'The last time I came, when I was with Paul,' she said with arch sweetness, 'we sat down there.' She leaned over and pointed with her thin Surbiton finger to the fifth row of the stalls, distant, indistinct, with toy people sitting in them.

'You get a better view up here,' I said sadly but stubbornly, and she replied something that I did not catch because the music began.

I leaned on the rail and, as ever, became lost in the splendid and lovely sounds that sometimes drifted, sometimes roared, from below. She sat upright, emitting little sniffing noises, and interrupting my dream by asking me if I would mind lighting her cigarette.

There was quite a bit of smoke coming up from below and she fanned herself irritably with the programme that I had purchased for a precious shilling. She did not read it, she just fanned her sharp little face with it.

I had just mentally placed the soloist in the piano concerto on the right hand of God, when she said quite loudly that she thought he sounded tinny, and when she came with Paul so-and-so was playing and he was bliss.

At the interval we sat fidgeting for a while before, as I had feared, she suggested that we went and had a drink. There was no escape now, no shoelace tying, no procrastination of any kind, for she was making smart little steps towards the bar.

Never in my life had I been in a bar of any sort. I knew from the films that you used various phrases to ask people what they would like to drink, and with a small satisfaction I remembered one from a picture we had seen at Dickies the previous Saturday.

'What's your poison?' I said, moving close to her and looking into her dark Surbiton eyes.

She giggled disconcertingly and said firmly: 'Gin and ton for me.'

I went to jelly. Gin and ton! Whatever it was, it sounded as though it cost quids. I would have to tell her, I just would, there was no going on with this.

But she smiled like sunshine before I could confess and she said: 'We'd better hurry, darling.'

Darling! This angel, with her high-heeled shoes and her gin and ton, had called me darling! Me with my yellow tie and my suit that not so long before I had worn for my bunk!

The endearment caught me up in a cloud and I staggered towards the bar. She was in love with me then. Girls didn't call you darling unless they were in love with you. All the time she had been hiding it, and doing it very well too.

And she called me that – and other people were standing around and they must have heard her saying it too. When people were in love in films they said that, but I did not think she would call me it. Darling!

I wondered if the woman at the bar had heard her. 'Gin and ton please, darling,' I said.

'Not so much lip,' she replied smartly, and I realised what I had said. 'Gin and tonic, is it and what else?'

My feet, both of them, were on the ground again now. 'Nothing else, thanks,' I whispered, 'I'm not drinking. How much is it?'

'You don't look old enough for a start,' she said, pouring the gin anyway. 'That will be one and eight.'

I returned to the girl bearing the gin and tonic as though it were a love potion. 'Gin and ton,' I said idly.

'Good,' she sniffed. 'Aren't you going to have something?'

'I'm on the wagon,' I said, feeling immediately pleased that the phrase tripped off so lithely. 'Football training, you know. We're not allowed to drink.'

'How boring,' she said, pouring the remainder of my one and eightpence down her red throat. 'Let's get back to this awful concert. Really, when I came with Paul . . .'

All the second half I crouched over the rail like a gargoyle, laden with despair now because I had realised that I did not have enough money to pay for our return fares. The music came up to mock me, and she sniffed audibly in the quiet passages, while I wondered what sort of a sensation I would cause by throwing myself into the chasm before me.

I had no serious intention of doing this, although I felt full enough of woe. The only way out of the mess, I decided, short of telling her that I came from Dickies, was to take her to Waterloo Station, buy her ticket and remember a sudden appointment on the other side of London.

The picture became composed in my mind and I became quite pleased with it. I would take her to the platform, kiss her softly but quickly, and like some strange agent or adventurer, would vanish into the crowd. She would sit on the train to Surbiton wondering about this mysterious man with whom she had become involved – well she did call me darling didn't she? – and I would try and walk home.

But I did not have even the satisfaction of this gallantry. We arrived at Waterloo and she produced a season ticket and said I need not bother to pay her fare. At least it saved me the walk. We sat stiffly, politely, on the train all the way to Surbiton in the rain. She had not called me darling again and I was feeling wretched. At Surbiton Station she fenced with the idea of getting a taxi, but like a glowing, fat angel on wheels a trolleybus flew around the corner and we boarded that instead.

We sat on top and presently she rose, announced that this was her stop, and held out a white limp hand that my heart must have resembled at that moment.

'Bye,' she said. 'Nice evening. See you.'

Then she had gone, jolting down the stairs, and out on to the rainy pavement, leaving me wrung out, disappointed, and cursing Dickies and the fate that made me belong to it. If I had taken her in the stalls like Paul, whoever he was, and given her plenty of gin and tons, and got a taxi from the station, it would have been different. We would have madly embraced in the taxi and then . . . oh hell, wasn't it murder with women!

By the time I had reached the dormitory I had grown a skin over the wound. 'What was it like?' asked Boz, his red nose sniffing over the sheet. He meant 'What was she like?'

but there was a certain code of ethics even among Dickie boys.

'Some women,' I said casually, taking off my boots, 'some of them drive you crackers. You should have seen this one, Boz. Went to the Albert Hall, drinks, and all that. She put away the gin and tons, I can tell you.'

'The what?' he said. 'What did she put away?'

'Gin and tons,' I said impatiently. 'Gin and tonics. They cost one and eightpence.'

'Jesus,' said Boz. 'One and eight! How much did it cost you altogether?'

'Quite a bit,' I said. 'Over a quid. But she was worth it.'

'I'll bet,' he grinned wickedly.

'Goodnight Boz,' I said, sliding down in bed.

' 'Night Monkey.'

'Don't call me that.'

'Why not?' he asked, genuinely surprised.

' 'Cos I don't like it,' I said. 'It's embarrassing.'

Last summer I went back to Dickies. To the satanic tower and the corridors jingling with memories. In one corner of the dining room, with generations of paint over them, it is true, are indents on the wall – the scoreboard of how many times Breadcrumb George swept the crumbs from the table into his mouth, in one week. There are eight little cuts there, made by Boz and I, showing it was a time of good gleaning for him.

Most things have changed now, of course. The formidable shell is the same, nothing but an earthquake could transform that, but inside there is no bleakness now. The dormitories are cut and divided into bedrooms, small bedrooms, and sitting rooms. There is a paddling pool, television all over the place, and a batch of sailing boats in which the boys adventure on the river. At the gate, the same old gate, I saw two boys returning from school, their heads cocked to music from a transistor set.

Long ago they took down the golden words from the front, so no one climbs along them any more. A plate on the front entrance informs the inquisitive passer by, or the arriving stranger, that this is Dr Barnardo's.

It was early May that I went last. A chilly day, an unwilling recruit to summer, the sort of day when you wonder whether the white fragments carried on the wind are snow or blossom.

The mudpatch is all black asphalt now, the churned battlefield of our days preserved like Pompeii beneath it.

But, standing at the centre, I see myself again there with the ball at my toe, waiting for the touch to Boz on my right to start the game. And again I see him pound through the mud, stockings hung over his boots, and with joy hitting the ball under, or over, or occasionally through the goalkeeper.

Or the mangy goat charging with terror and destruction on his horns, or the sprawling shade of the knobbly trees bruising the light brown summer dust, and me sitting reading on their fingered roots. One Sunday morning, with the pipe band crying and the Dickie boys marching and me at the window crying too, and hardly able to see the grand parade through my bitter, wet eyes.

And steamy Saturday nights in the gym when Frank Knights was in the projection room working the film, and the hero was about to put the heroine down on a terrible bed of straw. Then the Gaffer, leaping up and waving his arms into the beam of light, and shouting 'Stop it! Cut it off! No more of this filth!' And we would have to wait until the next Saturday and an uninterrupted showing of Abbot and Costello.

Every childhood is a meadow. Ours was stubbly and had weeds and stony places. But there was sweet grass too in patches, and days of sun and freedom and happiness. And, at its end, there was the gate to the Outside, and it opened for each of us, opened only once. Its notice, hung on its top bar, said: 'Shut The Gate Behind You,' which was an instruction as final as any.

Return as you might, Dickies was never yours again. Yours was the real world, to live in, to make fortunes, to die violently, or to remain in unremarkable sameness. To build visions and see them fulfilled, to journey far and to work and find joy and probably sorrow too.

The boys from Dickies did all these things in the after years. One married an heiress he met on a beach in Panama, one committed suicide, and one was in the newspaper because he threw stones at the underground train which killed his friend, his dog.

Boz and Bosky, Breadcrumb, Professor, Grandpa, Bug, Willie Dye, and Monkey too, as much as any of them, are shadows now. And the others too, with their thumping laughter, their dreams, whatever they might have been, and their joyous crimes of old. It was all a strange and wonderful misadventure.

Leslie Thomas
Onward Virgin Soldiers £2.95

Bustling with life and bawdy humour, National serviceman Brigg is
now a regular army sergeant defending the Empire in the beds and
bars of Hong Kong. Peace-time diversions include sensual fireworks
with a pair of delicious Chinese twins, and a tender, erotic affair with
the lonely wife of an American serviceman.

Orange Wednesday £2.99

The interior-sprung mattress took the excitement out of sex for
Prudence. Prudence took the excitement out of Lieutenant Brunel
Hopkins. Then she told him of Orange Wednesday . . .

Tropic of Ruislip £2.99

'A romp among the adulteries, daydreams and nasty woodsheds of
an executive housing estate . . . there are Peeping Toms, clandestine
couplings, miscegenation on the wrong side of the tracks, the
spilling of gin and home truths on the G-plan furniture, and the
steady susurrus of doffed knickers' GUARDIAN

'Extremely funny . . . for sheer pace, invention, gusto and accuracy,
Leslie Thomas takes some beating' SUNDAY TIMES

Tom Sharpe
The Great Pursuit £2.99

'Frensic . . . a snuff-taking, port-drinking literary agent . . . receives a
manuscript from an anonymous author's solicitor – "an odyssey of
lust . . . a filthy story with an even filthier style." Foreseeing huge
profits in the US, Frensic places the book with the Al Capone of
American publishing, Hutchmeyer, "the most illiterate publisher in
the world"' LISTENER

'The funniest novelist writing today' THE TIMES

The Wilt Alternative £2.99

The continuing saga of Henry Wilt, innate coward and hen-pecked
husband, whose unlikely escapades include a drunken – and very
painful – battle with a rosebush, an all-consuming infatuation with
a foreign student, and being an unwilling participant in a terrorist
siege . . .

'Sharpe is the funniest novelist currently writing . . . I sat curled up
with laughter' TIME OUT

Wilt on High £2.99

'Fans will relish the gamey imbroglio, complete with Peeping Toms
in the loo, comic American air-force officers and a herbalist whose
preparations, lacing Wilt's homebrew, induce an irrepressible
erection' OBSERVER

'He is the great post-Waugh humorist, the Wodehouse who dares
plunge into the bottomless vulgarity and hysteria of our times, and a
rattling good companion on a train journey' MAIL ON SUNDAY

Tom Sharpe
Blott on the Landscape £2.50

'Skulduggery at stately homes, dirty work at the planning inquiry, and the villains falling satisfactorily up to their ears in the minestrone ... the heroine breakfasts on broken bottles, wears barbed wire next to her skin and stops at nothing to protect her ancestral seat from a motorway construction' THE TIMES

'Deliciously English comedy' GUARDIAN

Wilt £2.99

'Henry Wilt works humbly at his Polytechnic dinning Eng. Lit. into the unreceptive skulls of rude mechanicals, but spends his nights in fantasies of murdering his gargantuan, feather-brained wife, half-consummated when he dumps a life-sized inflatable doll in a building site hole, and is grilled by the police, his wife being missing, stranded on a mud bank with a gruesome American dyke' GUARDIAN

'Superb farce' TRIBUNE

'... triumphs by a slicing wit' DAILY MIRROR

The Throwback £2.50

'The tale of an illegitimate member of the squirearchy earning his inheritance by increasingly nasty methods – gassing, suing, whipping, blowing up, killing, stuffing – is both inventive and pacy' NEW STATESMAN

'Black humour and comic anarchy at its best' SUNDAY TIMES

'A savage delight' DAILY MIRROR

All Pan books are available at your local bookshop or newsagent, or can be ordered direct from the publisher. Indicate the number of copies required and fill in the form below.

Send to: **CS Department, Pan Books Ltd., P.O. Box 40,**
             Basingstoke, Hants.   RG21 2YT.

or phone: 0256 469551 (Ansaphone), quoting title, author
             and Credit Card number.

Please enclose a remittance* to the value of the cover price plus: 60p for the first book plus 30p per copy for each additional book ordered to a maximum charge of £2.40 to cover postage and packing.

*Payment may be made in sterling by UK personal cheque, postal order, sterling draft or international money order, made payable to Pan Books Ltd.

Alternatively by Barclaycard/Access:

Card No. | | | | | | | | | | | | | | | | |

Signature:

Applicable only in the UK and Republic of Ireland.

While every effort is made to keep prices low, it is sometimes necessary to increase prices at short notice. Pan Books reserve the right to show on covers and charge new retail prices which may differ from those advertised in the text or elsewhere.

NAME AND ADDRESS IN BLOCK LETTERS PLEASE:

....

Name ——————————————————————————————

Address ——————————————————————————————

————————————————————————————————

————————————————————————————————

————————————————————————————————

3/87